The Fellowship of Life
Virtue Ethics and Orthodox Christianity

Moral Traditions & Moral Arguments
A SERIES EDITED BY JAMES F. KEENAN, S.J.

The Evolution of Altruism and the Ordering of Love
STEPHEN J. POPE

Love, Human and Divine: The Heart of Christian Ethics
EDWARD COLLINS VACEK, S.J.

Bridging the Sacred and the Secular:
Selected Writings of John Courtney Murray, S.J.
J. LEON HOOPER, S.J., editor

The Context of Casuistry
Edited by
JAMES F. KEENAN, S.J. and THOMAS A. SHANNON

Aquinas and Empowerment:
Classical Ethics for Ordinary Lives
Edited by
G. SIMON HARAK, S.J.

The Christian Case for Virtue Ethics
JOSEPH J. KOTVA, JR.

The Fellowship of Life
Virtue Ethics and Orthodox Christianity

Joseph Woodill

Georgetown University Press / Washington, D.C.

Georgetown University Press, Washington, D.C.
© 1998 by Georgetown University Press. All rights reserved.
Printed in the United States of America

10   9   8   7   6   5   4   3   2   1   1998

Library of Congress Cataloging-in-Publication Data

Woodill, Joseph.
    The fellowship of life : virtue ethics and Orthodox Christianity /
Joseph Woodill.
        p.   cm.—(Moral traditions & moral arguments series)
    Includes bibliographical references and index.
    1. Christian ethics—Orthodox Eastern authors. 2. Virtue.
3. Orthodox Eastern Church—Doctrines.   I. Title.   II. Series.
BJ1250.W59   1998
241'.4—dc21
ISBN 0-87840-700-6   98-13257

For Charlotte,
our children, and our parents

Contents

Editor's Preface

Moral Traditions & Moral Arguments, as a series, presents systematic, scholarly accounts of major themes in Christian ethics in order to critically examine those insights that, perduring through the ages, have shaped and continue to shape Christian lives and communities. These books are intended to provide scholars with a precise understanding of moral traditions as well as an appreciation of their contribution to contemporary life.

Weston School of Theology   JAMES F. KEENAN, S.J., ED.

Preface

People of virtue are more valuable than another book about virtue. They are also more helpful. In writing about virtue, I have been helped by many people. Here are but a few.

There would be no book without James F. Keenan, S.J. He not only guided me through a doctorate, but he showed me how to "cook" my work. I can still hear his words: "Joe, that's just awful." Whatever is good in this text is so thanks to Jim, while whatever is just awful is my fault.

Academics have professional colleagues to thank, but my formation has been more parochial. Not the university but church, family, wife, and children have formed me. I am grateful to the people of St. Michael's Church in Delaware and St. John's Church in New Jersey. I shared 18 years of my life with them. My parents, Joseph and Stephania, did all that they could to render me a person of Christian virtue before handing me over to Charlotte. It has been her blessing and cross to learn the love of God by loving one so unfinished as I. Our children have endured all of the rigors of being PKs. Pastors' Kids have a special cross to carry. When they read this, I hope that they better understand what we were trying to do with our lives.

Recently, Fr. Thomas Hopko the Dean of St. Vladimir's Seminary made it possible for me to teach ethics at the seminary as a guest lecturer. It was wonderful to spend time with the fine men and women studying at the seminary. I think that there truly is a "spirit of St. Vladimir's" that nourishes many Orthodox in America, and I am one so nourished. Without the books and the tireless speakers that have long issued from the seminary, I would have little to write about and understand even less.

I am also grateful for all of the help that I have received from Georgetown University Press, especially from the director John Samples.

1

Return to Virtue

In this book I want to consider Orthodox Christianity in light of the recent retrieval and revival of virtue ethics. The charting of virtue ethics and Orthodox Christianity will occur here at a number of levels, from contemporary virtue theorists, to the ancient Greek Fathers, to present Orthodox theologians, to contemporary applications. The final pages of the text will be devoted to locating and describing a workable virtue ethic as a resource from within the tradition of the Eastern Church. In charting the features of Orthodox Christianity in regard to virtue ethics, I will explain the importance of virtue for understanding the Eastern Church. My argument is that Orthodox Christianity is profoundly illumined by being conceived of as the pursuit of true virtue in Christ.

The beginning of the contemporary turn to virtue might be traced to an article published in 1958 by Elizabeth Anscombe. Anscombe's claim was that recent modes of doing ethics should be abandoned and that virtue should again become central to moral philosophy. [1] That article was soon joined by other philosophical critiques of contemporary ethics. Philippa Foot, who was also making important contributions at this time, wrote later that while the subject of virtue has been strangely neglected by moralists,

> things have recently been changing. During the past ten or fifteen years several philosophers have turned their attention to the subject, notably H.W. von Wright and Peter Geach. Von Wright devoted a not at all perfunctory chapter to the virtues in his book *The Varieties of Goodness* published in 1963, and Peter Geach's book called *The Virtues* appeared

---

Chapter 1 is a revision of "Virtue Ethics and Its Suitability for Orthodox Christianity," reprinted with permission from *St. Vladimir's Theological Quarterly* 41/1 (1997), 61–75.

in 1977. Meanwhile a number of interesting articles on the topic have come out in the journals. [2]

The dissatisfaction with contemporary ethics among philosophers was soon to be found among theologians. Gilbert Meilaender, a Lutheran ethicist, writes: "All around us are signs, if not of a revival in being virtuous, at least of a new interest in a theory of the virtues." [3] Meilaender claims that the widespread dissatisfaction with contemporary ethics seems centered in its "understanding of the moral life which focuses primarily on duties, obligations, troubling moral dilemmas, and borderline cases." [4] Meilaender maintains that a turn to virtue would encourage other considerations and a new understanding of ethics. For an ethic of virtue,

> *Being* not *doing* takes center stage; for what we ought to do may depend on the sort of person we are. What duties we perceive may depend upon what virtues shape our vision of the world. [5]

Paul Wadell, a Catholic ethicist, summarizes the sense of the inadequacy of recent ethics and the attraction of virtue ethics for theologians with these words:

> When we survey the literature today what we too often discover is not something to guide and instruct us, but an approach that does not go deep enough. What is missing is any normative sense of what being human entails. This is why we feel ethics so often misses the mark. We know morality involves becoming a certain kind of person. We know it entails a transformation of the self through habits and practices that work changes necessary for goodness. As Christians, we know the moral life is the spiritual life, the religious-sacramental life we have with God, a studied, ongoing attempt to establish ourselves as God's friends. [6]

Almost all of the desired features described above by Wadell were already in place as early as 1965 in a work by the Jewish theologian Abraham J. Heschel. Heschel published, in very few pages, a complete outline of what is, effectively, a virtue ethic in the book *Who Is Man?* Heschel establishes the "ought" that propels his ethic in the distinction and discontinuity between mere "human being" and the more of striving after "being human." There is to be found a logic, a practical reason, disclosed as one strives after being fully human. Heschel maintains that the proper categories to describe humanity must be practiced and, thereby, attained. Heschel insists that "to be human we must know what human being means, how to acquire, how to preserve it." [7] These are all questions of virtue: who we are, where we are going, and how to get there. [8]

Heschel's answer to how one might acquire and maintain the ought of "being human" is a number of sensibilities, modes of being, or, it would seem, virtues. Heschel maintains that "these features or sensibilities are no disparate trifles, random impressions, arbitrarily registered, but rather necessary components which constitute the essence of being human." [9] These are skills or excellences peculiar to the *telos* of humanity "within which man must be understood in his being human as distinguished from being animal, from being beastly" (31–32).

Some of these "features" of authentic human existence are preciousness, uniqueness, opportunity, and nonfinality. All of these modes are what we ought to be, but they must be acquired. Heschel writes:

> It is a fatal illusion to assume that to be human is a fact given with human being rather than a goal and an achievement. To animals the world is what it is; to man this is a world in the making, and being human means being on the way, striving, waiting, hoping (41).

These virtues are not acquired in solitude, according to Heschel: "Man alone is a conceit" (45). Community is absolutely necessary, as are models of wisdom. Heschel notes that one "always looks for a model or an example to follow" (8). For Heschel, as with Meilaender, "what determines one's being human is the image one adopts" (8).

Heschel summarizes his ethics by insisting that all of this points toward character education. "Life is clay, and character is form" (99). "Right living," Heschel insists, "is like a work of art, the product of a vision and of a wrestling" (99). This striving after the characteristics that allow right living will take place, necessarily, within a community of tradition, because, Heschel writes, "the authentic individual is neither an end nor a beginning but a link between the ages, both memory and expectation" (99).

Heschel might be described as but another philosopher of being as long as he seems to be describing being qua being, but his point is that having an "ought" at the center of human being indicates a prior requiredness. This is theology: "Theology asks about being as creation" (71). We strive, according to Heschel, after being human because there is a goal that comes with creation before the fact of being. Virtue is, then, a response to God's searching. Striving after what ought to be is inherent in Heschel's ethic, because God is in search of humanity.

Not unlike more recent virtue theorists, [10] Heschel holds that the problem is that "modern thinking has often lost its way by separating the problem of truth from the problem of living, cognition from man's total situation." [11] What would Heschel substitute for the confusion? He maintains that "the decisive form of human being is *human living.* Thus the proper theme for the study of man is the problem of living." [12] The confusion of contemporary morality stems, according to Heschel, from the attempt to derive "ought" from "is." Heschel claims:

> Against the conception of the world as something just here, the Bible insists that the world is creation. Over all being stand the words: Let there be! And there was, and there is. To be is to obey the commandment of creation. God's word is at stake in being. There is a cosmic piety in sheer being. What is endures as a response to a command. Philosophically the primacy of creation over being means that the "ought" precedes the "is." The order of things goes back to an "order" of God. [13]

This insistence that an "ought" precedes any grasp of what "is" is also central to the thought of Alasdair MacIntyre, arguably the most influential theorist in the recent revival of virtue ethics. [14] What we ought to become has to do with gaining virtues appropriate to a given end. MacIntyre—not unlike Heschel—thinks that the moral disarray of our age is due to the absence of a shared *telos* that would point to what ought to be. What modernity does have is a collection of ethical fragments of what remains to us after the traditions of virtue have been abandoned. It is MacIntyre's argument that after the traditions of virtue were rejected, "the language of morality passed from a state of order to a state of disorder." [15]

While the text *After Virtue* is MacIntyre's most often quoted book, he has held and traced an identifiable position since at least the 1966 publication of a history of ethics. The last chapter of that work laments the fact that modern moral philosophy begins with G.E. Moore's assertion that ethicists have heretofore simply been mistaken. It is Moore's claim that prior ethicists have been confused about good, i.e., that earlier thinkers supposed there to be some natural property termed "good"—which is, of course, Moore's famous "naturalistic fallacy." Here can be found, according to MacIntyre, the seeds of emotivism. Emotivism, as explained by MacIntyre, is the position "that the only authority which moral views possess is that which we as individual agents give to them." [16]

In contrast to a moral landscape made up of isolated individuals, maintaining incommensurable emotivist stances, MacIntyre would have us recover an ethics of virtue. [17] Such a recovery would entail that a community agree on its end or *telos*. The characteristic *telos* would entail virtues, skills, or excellences that would allow progress toward that end, all of which would have an institutionalized form that would shelter and preserve the structures of virtue. In a reversal of the usual and expected criticism, MacIntyre maintains that in such a community of virtue not only is moral criticism possible, but that in no other sort of community is there an established moral vocabulary that would allow for criticism of the sort that might allow for resolution. MacIntyre's position is that the interminable arguments of modernity are not simply because of profound differences, but because we have no common tradition that might adjudicate differences of interpretation.

In place of a moral landscape of unresolvable conflict, MacIntyre has attempted to describe what any community of virtue might require, although he seems not to have advanced the locating of any such vital community of virtue. The oft-quoted conclusion to *After Virtue* is a melancholic lament that we have no choice but to wait for the establishment of some such community. Stanley Hauerwas, in contrast, is certain that the searched-for community of virtue is Christianity. He has made it his task to describe Christianity as the concrete community that MacIntyre sought for in the abstract. Hauerwas has never written a book that did not credit MacIntyre with locating the fundamental notions that Hauerwas is attempting to incarnate.

Most of the books published by Hauerwas are collections of brief essays on a wide variety of subjects. There is no one book that describes his position comprehensively. There is, however, an essay that is particularly helpful in presenting a concise overview of the Hauerwas project. That essay is entitled "The Politics of Church: How We Lay Bricks and Make Disciples." It is an attempt to uncover and display the logical form of becoming a Christian in the light of MacIntyre's theoretical work.

MacIntyre has employed readily recognizable skills as analogies to bridge the epistemological gap and to indicate how becoming moral is like being apprenticed to a craft. Hauerwas suggests that an everyday practice such as bricklaying might help Christians think about what it means to be church. Learning to be a mason involves entering a tradition of skillfulness in a particular way, because no one learns bricklaying as if it were newly minted from the private world of the apprentice. Rather, one learns crafts—and, by implication, becomes virtuous—by being guided into the present state of a history or tradition of ends, goods, ways, and mentors. Hauerwas explains that

> bricks have different names—for example, klinkers—to denote different qualities that make a difference about how one lays them. These differences are discovered often by apprentices being confronted with new challenges, making mistakes, and then being taught how to do it by the more experienced. [18]

All of this talk about bricklaying harkens back, of course, to a central metaphor of MacIntyre's and Hauerwas applauds the clarity brought to ethics by MacIntyre's "extensive account of the craftlike nature of morality." [19] Hauerwas continues:

> MacIntyre argues that the moral good is not available to any intelligent person no matter what their point of view. Rather, in order to be moral, a person has to be made into a particular kind of person if he or she is to acquire knowledge about what is true and good. Therefore transformation is required if one is to be moral at all. [20]

The commitment to sanctification by transformation is not at all foreign to Reformation notions of Christianity, and Hauerwas is well within his tradition as a Methodist in insisting on it. However, Hauerwas maintains that such transformation is found primarily in worship and liturgy. [21] Hauerwas writes that "it is through liturgy [that] we are shaped to live rightly the story of God." [22]

Worship is, therefore, the practice that forms Christians, even as bricklaying forms proper bricklayers. Bricklayers ought to be seeking the goods that contribute to bricklaying, and, as such, are internal to that practice. Bricklayers may be corrupted when they form themselves to desired "goods" that are not essential to the craft of bricklaying. For example, bricklayers who want to make large sums of money by debasing their work at the behest of corrupt officials will soon find that they have damaged the craft and their ability to perform it. Hauerwas holds that any Christian community may likewise be debased by forming itself not for God, but for the world. The first classical instance of such debasement of Christian formation, according to Hauerwas, was in the fourth century when Constantine "honored" the church by offering it the "rewards" of political power. Just as the formation of good bricklayers is in sharp contrast to the formation required by corrupt officials, so Christianity as a community of virtue is always to be found in opposition to the world and its ability to form us. Hauerwas insists that a community "cannot help but be a social ethic, since it must stand in sharp contrast to the world which would have us build our relations on distortions and denials." [23]

The claim that a transformation is required in order to know the true and the good, so typical of the ethicists surveyed, is a theme that evokes strong resonance in Orthodox Christian thought. It is possible to uncover a deep and pervasive concern with the acquisition of true virtue by personal transformation in the Greek Fathers, the canonical exemplars of the tradition. From Athanasius the Great, to the Cappadocian Fathers, to Maximus the Confessor and John Climacus, the battle for the life in Christ is waged on the field of character and is won in virtue. [24] Maximus the Confessor, writing of the one who has grown mature in Christ, contends that "he creates through spiritual exercises the world of virtue as if this were some visible reality." [25] Athanasius ends the famous *On the Incarnation* with an appeal for all true believers to find their way into a correct understanding of the Scriptures by a transformation of the self wrought only by following the saints as exemplars into the "fellowship of life." [26] Jaroslav Pelikan maintains that the Cappadocians made "the doctrine of the *aretai* a recurring theme." [27] Pelikan notes that Gregory of Nazianzus, one of the Cappadocians, said of Athanasius that "in praising Athanasius, I shall be praising *arete*." [28] Pelikan emphasizes that by making this claim, Gregory of Nazianzus is managing to hold worship and virtue (*arete*) together. Pelikan notes that Gregory of Nazianzus maintained that "of all the *aretai*, none was more pleasing to God precisely as worship than the *arete* of showing mercy to others." [29] Gregory of Nyssa, another Cappadocian, the younger brother of Basil the Great, believed that the virtues "were the highest treasure to which human ambition could aspire." [30]

As if echoing the evident patristic concern with virtue and relating their concern to present attempts at a revival of virtue ethics, the Orthodox Christian ethicist Stanley Harakas writes that "Stanley Hauerwas comes close to the relationship of character and theosis in the Orthodox tradition." [31] This recognition is not at all surprising, inasmuch as Hauerwas has built his theological ethics on the foundation of the recovery of classical Greek ethics attempted by Alasdair MacIntyre. One might go so far as to say that they are retracing—if not replicating—the footsteps of Orthodox Christianity, but this is not to claim that they have taken all of the same turns or options. Because of the fundamentally classical elements embedded in the foundation of contemporary virtue ethics, it is attractive and useful to Orthodox Christianity. The key elements of this "classical" understanding are *telos*, practice, virtue, community, narrative, and mentoring. [32] Each of these elements will now be described in turn, especially as each relates to and is interdependent with the other

elements. As the six elements are described, I will suggest, further, why Orthodox ethicists will find them useful and compatible with Orthodox Christian
thought.

Telos is the first element to be considered. The recovery of ethics as
essentially teleological is basic to the work of virtue ethicists. They have
recovered the central question of any adequate virtue ethics: Who ought we
to strive to become? What is life's end? Both MacIntyre and Heschel insist
that the world is not simply made up of "facts" with an occasional ethical
dilemma, but that our life-world is permeated with ethical import. The world
is thoroughly colored by what ought to be.

This placing of an ought or *telos* at the center of the life-world is
attractive to Orthodox Christians. Stanley Harakas, writing about the is/ought
distinction made by the Cambridge Platonists, claimed that their "efforts failed
in part because they sought to embed their philosophy of the moral life in
an order outside the will of God. Is and ought are intertwined." [33]

Teleology is seen by Orthodox Christians to be buried in the very fabric
of human existence. Orthodox Christians have traditionally distinguished
between "image" and "likeness" in the biblical creation account to mean
"potential" and "striving." [34] Any account, therefore, that begins with what
ought to be, will be fundamentally attractive and useful to Orthodox Christians. For Orthodox Christians it is Christ who ought to be, i.e., who is willed
by the Father. God is our *telos*, to be found in Christ. The *telos* of human life
is not a private affair. The discernment, struggle, and acquisition of our end
is accomplished only within a community of practice and virtue.

Practice and virtue are the second and third essential elements of a
virtue ethic. A practice is formally defined by MacIntyre as "cooperative
human activity through which goods internal to that form of activity are
realized in the course of trying to achieve those standards of excellence which
are appropriate." [35] The Orthodox Christian notion of liturgy would suit
MacIntyre's notion of practice. Wayne Meeks, reflecting on MacIntyre, claims
that "ritual, within a functioning religious community, is paradigmatic
practice." [36] The importance of liturgy for Orthodox Christians is well-known.
What is less known is that Orthodox Christians consider liturgy to be as wide
as the church. "Church" itself is the fundamental practice within which more
specific liturgies are practiced. Constantine Cavarnos maintains that for the
Greek Fathers asceticism "embraces a whole well-organized way of life or 'life-
style'—one that takes into account the entire human being, soul and body, and
is followed throughout one's life, under the direction of a spiritual guide." [37]
Cavarnos, in the same place, equates *askesis* and practice. For Orthodox
Christians the "practice" of being mentored into a way of life in Christ, the

church, where the *telos* of transformation toward God in Christ might be accomplished, is fundamental.

Arete is the classical Greek term for "virtue" and is all but untranslatable. In tracing classical education and, so, virtue through ancient history, Marrou suggests that virtue is "the ideal value, to which life itself must be sacrificed." [38] *Arete* was for the ancients more likely to be grasped in a person than in a definition. *Arete* is best summed up as how one "lived and died in the effort to embody a certain ideal, a quality of existence." [39] The understanding of what that life was has varied through the ages; but a virtuous person remained the one who in the context of that life could be called "excellent." The difference between classical culture and Christianity is seen by Marrou as mainly one of a differing *telos*. While the final end of humanity varied in each school, the pedagogy was much the same. Marrou claims that the classical school for virtue never really came to an end, but was continued in the Greek Christian East. If this is so, and it seems to be, then a certain familiarity with the notions of virtue ethics should be expected among Orthodox Christians, insofar as they are inheritors of the "Greek Christian East." Marrou notes that "from 425 to 1453 the University of Constantinople was a most fruitful center of study, the main pillar of the classical tradition." [40]

A brief definition of virtue that would be intelligible from classical, to Christian, to modern times, would be "recognized standards of excellence." A formal definition of virtue presented by MacIntyre reads: "an acquired human quality the possession and exercise of which tends to enable us to achieve those goods which are internal to the practices and the lack of which effectively prevents us from achieving any such goods." [41]

With *telos*, practice, and virtue comes community, another essential element of virtue ethics. "It is always within some particular community with its own specific institutional forms," according to MacIntyre, "that we learn or fail to learn to exercise the virtues." [42] A communitarian turn seems to be central to virtue ethics. To enter into a practice in pursuit of some end or *telos* would be, MacIntyre asserts, "to subject my own attitudes, choices, preferences and tastes to the standards which currently define the practice." [43] Clearly, the focus of a virtue ethic as presented by MacIntyre shifts importance from the isolated individual to the community of believers. Orthodox Christians would, undoubtedly, agree with Wayne Meeks who holds that "we cannot begin to understand the process of moral formation until we see that it is inextricable from the process by which distinctive communities were taking shape. Making morals means making community." [44] Community is, then, the fourth essential element of virtue ethics that derives from and is intrinsically related to *telos*, practice, and virtue.

Narrative is yet another essential element for a virtue ethic. To restate the argument, virtue is that excellence, skill, or acquired characteristic expected of one who is appropriately formed in the wisdom of a community, as recovered by their stories. According to Wayne Meeks, MacIntyre and Hauerwas have staunchly maintained, that

> narrative is not merely a help for moral teaching—a relish to make the main dish go down easier, as Plutarch put it—but it is essential to proper moral reasoning. Moral discourse need not always be in the form of a narrative, but MacIntyre and Hauerwas argue that to be coherent and successful it must be connected with narrative. To speak of virtue entails that we tell stories. [45]

MacIntyre likewise convincingly contends:

> It is through hearing stories about wicked stepmothers, lost children, good but misguided kings, wolves that suckle twin boys, youngest sons who receive no inheritance but must make their own way in the world and eldest sons who waste their inheritance on riotous living and go into exile to live with the swine, that children learn or mislearn both what a child and a parent is, what the cast of characters may be in the drama into which they have been born and what the ways of the world are. Deprive children of stories and you leave them unscripted, anxious stutterers in their actions and their words. [46]

The last of the six elements is that of mentor. [47] As ancient as virtue ethics is the question, Can virtue be taught? David Hicks, in trying to recapture the ancient understanding of *paideia* (education for virtue) has observed that "no notable or influential ancient, it is fair to say, ever answered this question in the negative." [48] Virtue, then, can be taught, and the mentor is the one entrusted with that task. A mentor is one who must know, teach, and emulate the life of virtue. The mentor is the one who participates in virtue in such a way as to embody the tradition of virtue, linking past with future by guiding initiates.

For Orthodox Christians, the mentor is one who participates in Christ's teaching as a teacher. There is no figure more characteristic of Eastern Christianity than the elder as mentor. Orthodox Christian literature is full of figures of the *geron*, in Greek, or *starets*, in Russian. Starets Zossima, the mentor of Karamazov's son Aloysha, in Dostoyevsky's *The Brothers Karamazov*, is a typical Orthodox Christian mentor. The mentor is a necessary element of any virtue ethic, because such an ethic requires that we learn, or relearn, the language and ways of community and discipleship. The mentor and the pupil are the most elementary form of community outside of the natural community of family, which is not necessarily a community of virtue.

In summary, what remains, in its basic form, that might shape a virtue ethic? A virtue ethic must be able to establish a *telos* or end that would orient human life. The *telos* would be constitutive of the community or fellowship in pursuit of that end. The fellowship must maintain those practices that develop appropriate virtues in the acquisition of the fellowship's characteristic ends, all of which occur in a community advancing appropriate mentors who embody the narrative tradition. These fundamental elements, i.e., *telos*, practice, virtue, community, narrative, and mentoring can be exercised to orient our inquiry and to examine the Orthodox Christian tradition for a virtue ethic. Those elements will serve as a hermeneutic of virtue.

In the following pages I will continue to defend the apparent adequacy of virtue ethics for Orthodox Christianity. In chapter 2 I ask if traditional Patristic thought is concerned with virtue. My purpose is to establish a very basic topology of virtue in the vast corpus of works of the Fathers and, then, to select one Father in chapter 3 to more precisely locate aspects of the fundamental elements noted above. In chapter 3 I will consider *The Ladder of Divine Ascent* by John Climacus. In chapter 4 I select three Orthodox Christian ethicists and describe their approaches in order to uncover common and useful elements for my inquiry. Throughout these pages I relate the fundamental elements of *telos*, practice, virtue, community, narrative, and mentoring to the figures considered. The six fundamental elements noted are concerned with the process of Christian transformation. That transformation is from what is and moves toward what ought to be. The process is, necessarily, located between two poles. It moves, as noted above, between the poles of where we are and where we are going. Chapter 5 will serve to locate those poles more precisely. In chapter 5 I will first locate where we are coming from. That chapter will explain the Creation, the biblical Fall, and sin as Orthodox Christians understand them. It is, obviously, important to inquire into the Orthodox Christian understanding of the extent of the Fall—from "what ought to be" for humanity. The nature of sin, of *hamartia* or "missing the mark," will also be considered. Chapter 5 will also explore "what ought to be." I will contend in this chapter that the Orthodox Christian understanding of the movement from creation to redemption contains, inescapably, an implicit virtue ethic. In chapter 6 I will draw on all of the previous chapters to suggest the outline for an Orthodox Christian virtue ethic of marriage. Chapter 7 will serve to summarize what has been accomplished and will make a modest contribution to the contemporary discussion about virtue by distinguishing an Orthodox Christian virtue ethic from other recent models.

NOTES

1. G.E.M. Anscombe, "Modern Moral Philosophy," *Philosophy* 33 (January 1958): 1–19.

2. Philippa Foot, *Virtues and Vices and Other Essays in Moral Philosophy* (Berkeley: University of California Press, 1978), 1.

3. Gilbert C. Meilaender, *The Theory and Practice of Virtue* (Notre Dame: University of Notre Dame Press, 1984), 1.

4. Ibid., 4–5.

5. Ibid., 5.

6. Paul J. Wadell, *Friendship and the Moral Life* (Notre Dame: University of Notre Dame Press, 1989), 12.

7. Abraham Joshua Heschel, *Who Is Man?* (Stanford: Stanford University Press, 1965), 29.

8. Alasdair MacIntyre, *After Virtue: A Study in Moral Theory*, 2d ed., (Notre Dame: University of Notre Dame Press, 1984), 205, notes that "the unity of virtue in someone's life is intelligible only as a characteristic of a unitary life, a life that can be conceived as a whole."

9. Heschel, *Who Is Man?*, 31.

10. It is my suggestion that Heschel be considered a virtue ethicist. To my knowledge, no one has ever so identified Heschel.

11. *Who Is Man?*, 94.

12. Ibid., 95.

13. Ibid., 97.

14. An oft-rehearsed argument stemming from David Hume to G.E. Moore has been understood to conclude that the move from any fact to what ought to be is a fundamental mistake, a fallacy. The pertinent texts are David Hume, *A Treatise of Human Nature* published in 1739, especially Book 3, Part 1, which was added in 1740, and G.E. Moore, *Principia Ethica* (Cambridge: Cambridge University Press, 1903). In each of MacIntyre's major works there is a significant section devoted to the question of the relationship of "ought" to "what is." One should be willing, in any case, to grant MacIntyre that from a classical context "ought signified the presence of statable reasons that transcended personal preferences," according to Jeffrey Stout, *Ethics After Babel: The Language of Morals and Their Discontents* (Boston: Beacon Press, 1988), 204.

15. MacIntyre, *After Virtue*, 11.

16. Alasdair MacIntyre, *A Short History of Ethics* (New York: Collier Books, 1966), 264.

17. MacIntyre's claim is that contemporary moral argument is, for the most part, an emotivist mix of disconnected fragments, which is the argument of *After Virtue* and *A Short History of Ethics*. For MacIntyre, there are but three possible stances available to the post-Enlightenment person. These three are "Tradition," "Encyclopaedia," or "Genealogy." The first is characterized by being "limited" to the frame of a tradition, the second is characterized by the claim that one might stand in all traditions at once, the last is characterized by the claim that one need stand nowhere. The three would be represented by Aristotle, Kant, and Nietzsche. This last argument is the subject of Alasdair MacIntyre, *Three Rival Versions of Moral Enquiry: Encyclopaedia, Genealogy, and Tradition* (Notre Dame: University of Notre Dame Press, 1990). An

earlier book attempted to demonstrate that there is no universal rationality or notion of justice that might adjudicate these claims and, thus, we are forced either to the first or third stance. This is the argument found in Alasdair MacIntyre, *Whose Justice? Which Rationality?* (Notre Dame: University of Notre Dame Press, 1988).

18. Stanley Hauerwas, *After Christendom?* (Nashville: Abingdon Press, 1991), 102.

19. Ibid., 103.

20. Ibid.

21. The insistence on worship and liturgy as essential to ethics controls large portions of Hauerwas's ethics, and is a rather "unprotestant dictum" according to Robert W. Jenson, "The Hauerwas Project," *Modern Theology* 8 (July 1992): 285–295, at 290.

22. Stanley Hauerwas, *Christian Existence Today* (Durham, North Carolina: The Labyrinth Press, 1988), 107.

23. Ibid., 103.

24. A classic description of the struggle where possession of virtue is to win the battle is found in *John Climacus: The Ladder of Divine Ascent*, trans. Colm Luibheid and Norman Russell, Introduction by Kallistos Ware, *The Classics of Western Spirituality: A Library of the Great Spiritual Masters* (New York: Paulist Press, 1982), 236 (step 26).

25. *Maximus the Confessor: Selected Writings*, trans. George C. Berthold, *The Classics of Western Spirituality: A Library of the Great Spiritual Masters* (New York: Paulist Press, 1985), 142 (*Chapters on Knowledge*, First Century 79).

26. Athanasius, *On the Incarnation*, trans./ed. A Religious of C.S.M.V. (New York: St.Vladimir's Theological Seminary, 1953), 96 (*De Incarnatione* 57). The passage is rendered as "included in their company through the manner of his life" (p. 257) in *Contra Gentes and De Incarnatione*, trans./ed. Robert W. Thomson (Oxford: Clarendon Press, 1971); it is translated as "associated with them in the conduct of a common life" (p. 67) in *Athanasius: Select Works and Letters*, in *A Select Library of Nicene and Post-Nicene Fathers of the Christian Church*, Second Series, vol. 4 (Peabody, Massachusetts: Hendrickson Publishers, Inc., 1994).

27. Jaroslav Pelikan, *Christianity and Classical Culture* (New Haven: Yale University Press, 1993), 141.

28. Ibid., 307 (*Oration* 21.1).

29. Ibid., (*Oration* 14.5).

30. Ibid., (*De virginitate* 4).

31. Stanley Harakas, *Toward Transfigured Life: The Theoria of Eastern Orthodox Ethics* (Minneapolis: Light and Life Publishing Company, 1983), 183.

32. These elements are "classical" in that they recur of necessity in all of the ethicists, from ancient to modern, that we will consider.

33. Stanley Harakas, "The Natural Law Teaching of the Eastern Orthodox Church," *The Greek Orthodox Theological Review* 9 (Winter 1963–64): 215–224, at 224.

34. The Septuagint version of the Scriptures as used by the Greek Church reads Genesis 1.26–27 as *eikon* and *homoiosis*. As understood by the Eastern Church, these words indicate participation in and striving toward a *telos* as essential elements of salvation. This distinction comes from Irenaeus of Lyon and is a commonplace in Orthodox piety. The anthropology of image and likeness is understood by the Orthodox

to be the golden thread uniting the whole of the faith. Any ethic would need to be able to account for this, if it is to be employed by the Orthodox believers. John Meyendorff, *Byzantine Theology: Historical Trends and Doctrinal Themes* (New York: Fordham University Press, 1979), 139, explains that "the 'natural' participation of man in God is not a static givenness; it is a challenge and man is called to *grow* in the divine life." Meyendorff concludes that salvation is, indeed, a gift, but, just as essentially, it is also a task and we must strive after it.

35. *After Virtue*, 187. MacIntyre suggests that some common sorts of practice would be architecture, football, and farming.

36. Wayne Meeks, *The Origins of Christian Morality: The First Two Centuries* (New Haven: Yale University Press, 1993), 91.

37. Constantine Cavarnos, *The Hellenic-Christian Philosophical Tradition* (Belmont, Massachusetts: Institute for Byzantine and Modern Greek Studies, 1989), 55–56.

38. Henry I. Marrou, *A History of Education in Antiquity*, trans. George Lamb (Madison: The University of Wisconsin Press, 1956), 11.

39. Ibid.

40. Ibid., 340.

41. *After Virtue*, 191.

42. Ibid., 194–95.

43. Ibid., 190.

44. *Origins of Christian Morality*, 5.

45. Ibid., 189.

46. *After Virtue*, 216.

47. The word "mentor" derives from what is, perhaps, one of the oldest texts in the history of education in virtue. It comes from Homer's *Odyssey*. Mentor is the friend of Odysseus who was entrusted to care for Telemacus, the king's son.

48. David V. Hicks, *Norms and Nobility: A Treatise on Education* (Savage, Maryland: Rowman and Littlefield, Inc., 1991), 22.

2

The Fellowship of Life: The Fathers on Virtue

The Orthodox Christian ethicist Stanley Harakas has written that "though most people who have some knowledge of Eastern Orthodox Christianity may have some appreciation for its liturgical tradition, spirituality, dogmatic formulations, or sense of tradition, few have looked to Eastern Orthodoxy as a source of ethical teaching." [1] He concludes that this is so because it was not until very recently—not until after the revolution in Greece in 1821—that systematic studies in ethics first appeared among Orthodox theologians. Harakas notes that the early period of Eastern Orthodox thought was primarily concerned with dogma and the formulations of faith concerning the person of Jesus Christ. And, in any case, "the sorts of concerns which are the subject matter of investigation for the modern day ethician were not often dealt with by Eastern Orthodox writers, at least not in the manner to which we have been accustomed in our times." [2] Harakas concludes by claiming that "one will search in vain in the writings of the Church Fathers for systematic treatments of Orthodox Christian ethics." [3]

The reason that the writings have been searched in vain is because, when they are examined, there emerges an ethic centered on the acquisition of virtue. It is, as Harakas claims, not what most contemporary ethicians would be accustomed to find; neither is it "systematic" in the sense that ethics becomes divorced from the rest the body of Christian belief and understanding. It is an ethic that accepts, with reservations, the inheritance of the Greek notion of excellence and a fundamental concern with virtue, but with the added awareness that the Christian *telos* points beyond mere human excellence toward the excellence or virtue of Christ.

A complete survey of all of the Patristic literature of the Eastern Church is far beyond the scope of this chapter. I will consider only a limited—but highly representative—portion of the Patristic inheritance. Any list of the most important Eastern Church Fathers, however short, would undoubtedly include Athanasius the Great, the Cappadocian Fathers, [4] and John Chrysostom. These Fathers will be considered to establish my claim that virtue is an essential element in Patristic thought. I hope to show that a concern for the acquisition of virtue is both fundamental and central to their thought. I am convinced, however, that if an extended examination were undertaken, it would serve to show a virtual identification of ethics with virtue in Eastern Patristic authors.

ATHANASIUS

Athanasius the Great (c. 295–373) was "one of the most imposing figures in all ecclesiastical history." [5] He was the foremost defender of the theology formulated at the Council of Nicea held in 325. The Arians saw Athanasius as their primary enemy and did everything possible to harm him. "Five times was he banished from his episcopal see and spent more than seventeen years in exile." [6] "The Greek Church called him later 'the Father of Orthodoxy,' whereas the Roman Church counts him among the four great Fathers of the East." [7]

Athanasius's *On the Incarnation* is an argument for the necessity of God's incarnation, if humanity is to be saved. The oft-quoted declaration that God became human "that we might become divine" [8] is the conceptual center of the work. In that text we encounter the intimation that virtue is necessary even to gain a right understanding of Scripture. For Athanasius, truth, its understanding, and the problem of right living are all intimately connected. One needs Christian virtue as a guide, and such virtue is only acquired by being mentored into the way of the saints. By imitating the exemplars of the faith, one can hope to be transformed. Such a transformation results in a common understanding. This ontological union in virtue is called by Athanasius a fellowship, the company of the saints.

Attaining the fellowship of life is communion in—and by virtue of—Christ, who is the new and excellent humanity. According to Athanasius, God is life. Turning away from the God who is life has brought death and corruption into God's creation. In order to overcome the separation of humanity from God and, so, life—which is the *telos* of humanity—the Word of God the Father took a body like our own and surrendered to the Father in perfect obedience. Athanasius contends that

> this he did in his loving kindness in order that, as all die in him, the
> law concerning corruption in men might be abolished—since its power
> was concluded in the Lord's body and it would never again have influence

over men who are like him—and in order that, as men had turned to corruption, he might turn them back again to incorruption and might give them life for death, in that he had made the body his own, and by the grace of the resurrection had rid them of death as straw destroyed fire. [9]

So, Christ "rid us of death and renewed us." [10] All attempts to live life well are limited by humankind's separation from true life, i.e., from God. Thus, the pursuit of virtue outside of Christ is never quite successful. Without God Incarnate, we do not know our end; neither will we have understood the scriptural narratives. And, therefore, we cannot gain true virtue by any practice that is outside the fellowship of life, outside the knowledge of our proper end. For Athanasius, salvation in Christ brings with it the possibility of attaining our true and appropriate end. Only within the community of life can true virtue or excellence be attained. The life in Christ *is* virtue. In Christ is human excellence accomplished. Athanasius writes that "a more perfect instruction in virtue one could not find than that which the Lord typified in himself." [11] It is clear that Athanasius understands the Christian task in terms of the classical search for virtue. One must attain virtue or excellence by gaining entry into a community that knows the proper *telos* of life and that harbors appropriate mentors. What of practices and narratives?

In *The Letter to Marcellinus*, Athanasius insists that "the entire Holy Scripture is a teacher of virtues." [12] It is not enough, however, simply to read or know the Scriptures. They must be performed aright, i.e., practiced. The Psalms, according to Athanasius, are the perfect practice for the one who intends to gain the virtues of the saints. Athanasius claims that when the Psalms are celebrated correctly, [13] they form one in harmony with the spirit of the Scriptures as found in the saints. It is the practical formative function of the Psalms, the ability to order aright one's character with that of the saints, that is the particular grace of the Psalms. Psalms are transformative as the enacted or practiced narrative of what God would have us become in Christ. Athanasius makes clear that this life in virtue is not at all the individual's expression of private religious sentiment; it is, rather, a corporate enterprise where one is shaped and formed by community worship, to be made an adequate representative of the "fellowship of life." Using a music metaphor, he sees the music of worship playing us and not us it. [14] "As in music," Athanasius suggests, "there is a plectrum, so the man becoming himself a stringed instrument and devoting himself completely to the Spirit may obey in all his members and emotions, and serve the will of God." [15] Therefore for Athanasius, communal worship "sings" us; and the practice of worship forms the whole person, including one's affections. [16] Athanasius ends the letter with reassurance that what Marcellinus needs to do is to practice the work of a bishop, especially the Psalms. Do this, he writes, "and the kind of life the holy, God-bearing men possessed who spoke these things—this life you also shall imitate." [17]

If God has loved humanity enough to become incarnate, then there must always be those like Athanasius to show us the way to the life of Christian virtue. Athanasius' own mentor and exemplar of the holy, God-bearing man is surely Anthony of Egypt. At the close of *The Life of Anthony*, Athanasius notes that those such as Anthony want only to live humbly and do not want to be singled out as mentors. However, since God has not forgotten but remains with us, "the Lord shows them like lamps to everyone, so that those who hear may know that the commandments have power for amendment of life, and may gain zeal for the way of virtue." [18]

Ellen Charry is surely correct in locating the "aretology" of Athanasius at the very center of his thought, unifying the whole of his theology. "Aretology" is, according to Charry, the dynamics "of the formation of human excellence at God's direction." [19] Charry notes that Athanasius understands that human beings "strive to reproduce what they admire. The trick is to be sure that the object of admiration is apt." [20] Athanasius presents Christ as the archetypal exemplar of virtue in whom the *telos* of godlikeness is fully realized. To become like God in Christ is to acquire his virtues, which would include the virtue of ministering this fellowship to others. If God comes to give his life in fellowship to us, then those who have acquired his virtue must, in fellowship, also guide others into God's life. We are formed in virtue by the gift of God himself in Christ, and we are so formed when we—like Anthony, Athanasius, or others in the "fellowship of life"—give ourselves graciously to others. Athanasius writes that

> although there be one Son by nature, true and only-begotten, we too become sons, not as He in nature and truth, but according to the grace of Him that called, and though we are men from the earth, are yet called gods, not as the True God or His Word, but as has pleased God who has given us that grace; so also, as God do we become merciful, not by being made equal to God, not becoming in nature and truth benefactors ... but in order that what has accrued to us from God Himself by grace, these things we may impart to others, without making distinction, but largely towards all extending our kind service. For only in this way can we anyhow become imitators, and in no other, when we minister to others what comes from Him. [21]

There is to be found in Athanasius, as Charry detected, a union of theoretical and practical theology precisely in the area and importance of virtue. That we can acquire the virtues characteristic of God is possible, because God has become like us; and God has become like us, so that we might find no impediment to the life of true virtue. This is not unlike the function of virtue in the Cappadocian Fathers, to be considered next.

THE CAPPADOCIANS

It was not before the middle of the fourth century "that the province of Cappadocia produced three great theologians, Basil of Caesaria, his friend Gregory Nazianzus and his brother Gregory of Nyssa whom we shall call 'the three great Cappadocians.' " [22] J. Quasten concludes that "in this splendid triad the theological work of Athanasius found its continuation and reached its climax." [23] The Cappadocians completed the defeat of Arianism begun by Athanasius.

The works of the Cappadocians are replete with references to virtue and its importance. One finds Gregory Nazianzus in the heat of theological debate defending himself against another's calumny by writing that "he would despise being held in high esteem by anyone who is not really a virtuous man." [24] Gregory of Nyssa paraphrases Athanasius when he maintains that the one seeking "virtue participates in nothing other than God, because he is himself absolute virtue." [25] The parents of Basil the Great were praised by Basil's friend Gregory of Nazianzus because their marriage was an icon in "common esteem of virtue no less than in body." [26] Basil's entire family remained "teachers of virtue" even in persecution, as described by Gregory of Nazianzus. [27] All of this comes from a Christian funeral oration that is described as having for its purpose the gratification of "admirers of virtue," and to be an "inspiration to virtue" concerning one who was "a norm of virtue for all." [28] It is difficult to find a passage in the Cappadocians that does not make reference to the life of virtue in classical terms and language. This is because the Cappadocian Fathers "stood squarely in the tradition of Greek culture." [29] This is not to say that they were not critical of that culture—they were; however, they were so steeped in classical modes of thinking, that it is difficult to divorce their thought on the place of virtue and morality from their faith. Jaroslav Pelikan notes that virtue was, indeed, a recurring theme for the Cappadocians. He observes that their "very way of treating the issue suggested their dependence on Classical models" (141). It is this dependence on classical modes of thinking that is the subject of Pelikan's book. His exposition will aid our recovery of the importance of virtue in Eastern Church thought and, in particular, in the Cappadocian Fathers.

Pelikan's *Christianity and Classical Culture* is an attempt to analyze the specifics of "natural theology" in the thought of the Cappadocian Fathers. It is Pelikan's argument that the natural theology of the Greek Christian tradition is a product of the encounter between Christianity and Hellenism. Much is found in this encounter to be acceptable to Christianity by the Cappadocians, but there was also much that they rejected and were critical of in Greek thought. Pelikan notes that while the Cappadocians aligned themselves with Greek natural philosophy, "yet they found no positive connection between the sacramental mysteries over which they were presiding and the pagan 'mysteries,' even though these did bear some similarities to the Christian ritual" (23). The Cappadocian Fathers both revered the Greek cultural pursuit of virtue found for example in Homer and Hesiod and, yet, despised the myths presented in the same works.

While Greek religious practice was rejected, the natural philosophy of Greek thought could be joined to Christian life. "Therefore, the parallels between this 'natural philosophy' and this 'more sublime life'—that is, between Classical ethical theory and Christian ethical theory—as well as the contrasts between Christian moral behavior and Classical immoral behavior, could be mined for their apologetic value" (30). Christian and Greek ethics had, according to Pelikan, much in common, as understood by the Cappadocians. The Cappadocians used this similarity both as an "apologetic," i.e., to establish their own Christian position in terms reasonable to educated Greeks, and as a "presupposition," i.e., to refute the inadequacy of Greek religion once the standards had been granted. As such, the Cappadocians seem to have taken a stance that Greek virtue ethics is correct in form, i.e., the pursuit of human excellence, but that Greek society might be reproved for the failure to attain the human *telos* and this because of the superiority of Christianity as the repository of the true end of humanity. "For all the parallelism in ethical theory," Pelikan observes, "Cappadocian apologetics was always ready to point out the glaring inconsistency between Classical theory and Greco-Roman practice, notably in the area of sexual morality, while acknowledging also that Christian practice also fell short of the ideal" (31). Pelikan concludes that however congenial to Greek thought they were, the Cappadocians kept dogmatics and apologetics together. It would seem that while there could be a typology of virtue that was shared by all, the content of such virtue language was dependent on differences such as *telos* and doctrine. For instance, Gregory of Nyssa, Pelikan observes, begins his *Catechetical Oration* by asserting "the need of a system of instruction" (31). The need was felt because, in spite of all of the parallels with Greek ethical theory, there is the moral requirement, again according to Gregory of Nyssa, to "be weaned away from all experience of evil" (31).

No single work by one of the Cappadocians would better illustrate their relationship to classical Greek ethical theory than "Address to Young Men on Reading Greek Literature" by Basil the Great. In that letter Basil writes to students who "each day resort to teachers and hold converse with the famous men of the ancients through the words which they have left behind." [30] He asks that each one of them hesitate before surrendering to these famous men "the rudders of your mind, as if of a ship" (381 [*Ad adolescentes*, sect. 1]). He also has a lesson to teach them, and it will enable them to distinguish what is and what is not useful about Greek *paideia*.

Basil is directing his students to consider the "end" of any study. Nothing is of value that does not contribute to the *telos* of life lived for God.

> Neither renown of ancestry, nor strength of body, nor beauty, nor stature, nor honors bestowed by all mankind, nor kingship itself, nor other human attribute that one might mention, do we judge great, nay, we do not even consider them worth praying for, nor do we look with admiration upon those who possess them, but our hopes lead us forward to a more distant time, and everything we do is by way of preparation for the other life (381–383 [2]).

We are to pursue vigorously only what contributes to the end of Christian life. Christian *eudaimonia*, Basil asserts in the same place, is described in the Holy Scriptures and taught in the sacramental mysteries. Therefore in considering Greek *paideia*, one must distinguish the *telos*, the narrative, and the practice.

Basil concedes that young minds may fail to grasp the depth of his lesson and, so, he will resort to figures of speech. He suggests that training the "eye of the soul" be compared to military basic training. Every Christian faces "a contest, the greatest of all contests" (385). Basil demands that a sort of basic training be done in preparation for the Christian struggle that is before us. Greek education is a sort of Christian basic training. Therefore, we "must strive to the best of our power, and must associate with poets and writers of prose and orators and with all men from whom there is any prospect of benefit" (385). Christians are like "cloth" about to be dyed. The craftsmen who color fabric must prepare the material by coloring it first with some similar hue and only then do they attempt to fix the final pigment. A third illustration is immediately appended and Basil suggests that one might see

Greek *paideia* as like "seeing the reflection of the sun in water" (385). Greek *paideia* is to Basil a matter of basic preparation for Christianity, and he will show that there is "some affinity between the two bodies of teaching" (385 [3]). At the very least, Greek learning, while not the "fruit" of Christian life, is a valued part of the "tree." We may conclude that Basil does not doubt the usefulness of Greek education for the Christian spirit, but he has yet to explain just how to participate in it.

The poets, according to Basil, are to be engaged when they present narratives of those who are striving for what is good. When the wicked are glorified in the Greek poets, Christians ought not to have ears because "familiarity with evil words is, as it were, a road to evil deeds" (389 [4]). Narratives, according to Basil, have great power to form a person. He suggests that narratives about gods behaving like beasts ought not to be considered seriously. These guidelines are not limited only to poets, but are also intended to judge prose works made to entertain.

Wherever the Greek writers are found to be praising virtue, there Christians ought to be, Basil insists, like bees to the honey (391). This is the very heart of the matter. What is valuable is the very notion of virtue that may be gleaned from Greek *paideia*. Basil explains that

> since it is through virtue that we must enter upon this life of ours, and since such has been uttered in praise of virtue by poets, much by historians, and much more still by philosophers, we ought especially to apply ourselves to such literature. For it is no small advantage that a certain intimacy and familiarity with virtue should be engendered in the souls of the young, seeing that the lessons learned by such are likely, in the nature of the case, to be indelible, having been deeply impressed in them by reason of the tenderness of their souls (393 [5]).

There is no doubt that the value of virtue for the good life is the key to Basil's appreciation for Greek *paideia*. In praising *Works and Days*, Basil notes that Hesiod

> has narrated these things for no other reason than to urge us on to virtue and to exhort all men to be good, and to keep us from becoming weak and cowardly in the face of the toils and desisting before reaching the end. And assuredly, if anyone else has sung the praise of virtue in terms like Hesiod's, let us welcome his words as leading to the same end as our own (395).

Included in Basil's carefully limited applause of Hesiod and Homer is Solon. He also may be read as one who taught that we ought to cling to virtue. Wealth falls away, riches change by day, but virtue, Solon teaches, is the only wealth that endures. Xenophon is also to be valued. Heracles is presented by him as being offered virtue and vice. Vice comes offering immediate satisfaction, while virtue is presented as a worthy love offering sweat and labor but her prize is "to become a god" (399).

Praise of virtue is good but it is not enough. Basil requires harmony with what is worthy of praise. He maintains that the true musician would not play an instrument that is out of tune, neither should a student of virtue settle for mere praise of virtue while being "out of tune" with it. Praising or speaking of virtue while not being virtuous is, according to Basil, like playing an out-of-tune lyre because the end of virtue is a kind of life. The student of virtue is being "tuned" to a proper *telos*. Further in the text, Basil contends that music is to be taken very seriously by the students. There is a "difference between giving full ear to wholesome and to licentious music" (419 [9]). As with Athanasius, Basil sees music as being morally significant to formation in virtue.

Not only virtue but Greek understandings of *telos* may have some similarity to the Christian forms. Basil commends, among others, Socrates and Pericles whose "examples tend to nearly the same end as our own" (405 [7]). It seems to Basil that none of this similitude is mere chance. These are all excellent examples in Greek thought, he claims, of a proper notion of end as necessarily gained by the trial of virtue. Since Christians are also, so to speak, navigators, archers, and craftsmen striving after a proper end to our craft, we ought not fall behind these other artisans of the spirit, at least in respect to learning how to recognize what is in our own interests. "For can it be," Basil asks, "that handicraftsmen have some end in view in their work, but that there is no goal for the life of man, keeping his eye upon which that in man at least, who does not intend to be wholly similar to the brute beasts, ought to do and say whatever he does or says?" (409 [8]).

In short, preparation of the sort that might be gained by Greek *paideia* is not wasted. In sport or in music, Basil observes, you must practice for the crown of victory. Practice must always be appropriate to its end, Basil insists, and any proper practice is valuable. Practice gives one the capacity to complete a contest and not quit before the end. How these pagans struggle for a mere crown of wild olive, Basil wonders, while Christians who might win the greatest crown of all waste their hours (411–413).

What then were some of the elements that the Cappadocians were willing to retain of classical virtue ethics? The Cappadocians never questioned the function of *telos* in Greek virtue ethics. Pelikan is surely correct to claim that the Cappadocians accepted "the valid intuition that behind the changes and chances of this moral life there was some meaning or purpose." [31] Living has a goal and that goal is the *telos* established in creation. Basil asks if it can be the case that navigators, archers, and other handicraftsmen have an end, but that the crafting of life itself has no goal?

A major thread of Pelikan's argument is that while the Cappadocians aligned themselves with much in classical Greek thought, they rejected the importance of the notions of "chance" and "necessity." Our *telos* is not a matter of any caprice, nor is it a necessity of any fate. It was not necessity or chance "that decided the direction of human lives" (159). According to Pelikan, virtue was for the Cappadocians a matter of free choice. Pelikan notes that Gregory of Nyssa maintained that "*arete* is a voluntary thing, subject to no dominion: that which is the result of compulsion and force cannot be *arete*" (160). For the Cappadocians, to understand virtue is to reject randomness and to affirm a divine teleology. This divine teleology is dynamic and ceaseless. Pelikan summarizes by explaining that

> both the comprehensive range and the fixed limitations of natural theology were expressed in this teleology of the vision of God, so much of which could be known by enlightened reason, so much more of which could be known only by grace, still more of which could be learned only gradually in an eternal quest without satiety, and infinitely more of which remained forever unfathomable in the transcendent mystery of divine nature that was knowable only in its unknowability (165).

Pelikan concludes that for the Cappadocians, "the traditional *aretai* of Greek ethical thought applied to Christian ethics, too" (197). The moral presuppositions of Greek thought were the most "natural" and least questionable elements to be encountered by the Cappadocians, which explains the free range that these notions are given in Cappadocian writings. "Celebrated by Plato and Aristotle," Pelikan summarizes,

> *arete* represented a distinctive Greek principle. Therefore, it was possible for the Cappadocians to take the Greek understanding of *arete* for granted as a presupposition in dealing with either pagans or Christians (196).

We may be certain that not only was virtue in the classical sense important and foundational to the Cappadocians, but it formed an essential and fundamental part of the structure of what is known as "natural law" in the Christian East.

JOHN CHRYSOSTOM

John Chrysostom was one of "the four great Fathers of the East." [32] He was born (c. 344–345) in Antioch of an aristocratic and wealthy family. After baptism he left Antioch to join a group of Christian ascetics, but the rigorous life forced him to return home. Returning to Antioch, he was ordained a deacon by Meletus in the year 381 and a priest in 386 by Bishop Flavian. Flavian appointed John to preach at the city's major church for twelve years. It was here in Antioch that the preacher so identified with Constantinople gained the reputation of being "Chrysostom," i.e., "golden mouthed." His life changed dramatically when Nectarius, the patriarch of Constantinople, died and John was chosen to succeed him. John Chrysostom's attempts to reform a corrupt clergy met with resistance. After being exiled a number of times, he died on 14 September 407. His body was brought back to Constantinople in solemn procession on 27 January 438, and interred in the Church of the Apostles. [33] No Greek Father has left a larger body of literature than Chrysostom. [34]

In the introduction to a collection of John Chrysostom's most significant sermons on marriage and family life, Catharine Roth notes that while matters of high theology dominated the works of the great Fathers such as St. Athanasius of Alexandria, St. Basil of Caesaria, St. Gregory Nazianzus, and St. Gregory of Nyssa, "the practical problems arising for Christian life in a pagan society were the primary concerns of St. John Chrysostom." [35] Roth maintains that John Chrysostom's "main theme is that marriage is intended to promote virtue" (21). We will consider his promotion of virtue in two areas: spousal virtue and the virtue of children.

It is clear that for John Chrysostom marriage is good. "How foolish," he claims, "are those who belittle marriage" (55 [*Ephesians,* homily 20]). After all, he notes, "if marriage were something to be condemned, Paul would never call Christ a bridegroom and the Church a bride, and then say this is an illustration of a man leaving his father and his mother, and again refer to Christ and the Church" (55). For our purposes, however, it is important to note that not only is marriage good, but it is the ecclesial locus for the formation of virtue. It is, for Chrysostom, a "small church." (Chapter 6 of this volume will discuss at length an Orthodox Christian virtue ethic of marriage.) Marriage is itself a practice or mystery through which we may become fit Christians, growing in virtue. In marriage, according to

Chrysostom, "it is possible for us to surpass all others in virtue by becoming good husbands and wives" (57).

Virtue takes precedence over all other purposes for marriage. While children are among the ends of marriage, John Chrysostom holds in a homily on 1 Corinthians 7.2 that now—in the fourth century—"the whole world is filled with our kind" (85 [*Sermon on Marriage,* homily 20]). Children were desirable as a memorial before the coming of Christ, but because of Christ, death is overcome by the Resurrection. Children are seen by Chrysostom as having been given by God as a comfort to a world that needed "images of the departed and to preserve our species. For those who were about to die and for their relatives, the greatest consolation was their offspring" (85). Christians, however, are not formed for death but for life. Christians practice for and pursue the virtues of the kingdom; they are not in pursuit of virtues to complement a life that will end. For Christians, seeking after "posterity is superfluous. If you desire children, you can get much better children now, a nobler childbirth and better help in your old age, if you give birth by spiritual labor" (85–86). Human excellence or virtue is an ontological rebirth and not the mere continuation of the species.

Having limited reproduction as a lesser purpose for Christian marriage, Chrysostom claims that its purpose is to avoid vice and to attain to the virtues of chastity and holiness. Only the common pursuit of virtue can sustain true marriage. "Just as a virtuous man can never neglect or scorn his wife," claims Chrysostom, "so a wanton and licentious man can never love his wife, no matter how beautiful she is" (88). This is so because, according to Chrysostom, only "virtue gives birth to love" (88). Chrysostom maintains, then, that the purpose of marriage is to practice and gain the virtue of chastity. "To this end," he requires that, "every marriage should be set up so that it may work together with us for chastity" (99 [*How to Choose a Wife*]). How Christian marriage is made to be "set up" and "work" with the church for virtue can best be seen in three areas: in the spousal search and selection, in the wedding celebration, and in regard to sexuality.

In searching out a spouse, John tells his listeners, "you rush eagerly to the experts in civil law. You sit beside them and question them carefully" (89). This is, he claims, because we fear to lose money to a bad marriage. Ought we not as Christians to be more concerned to seek out those who are wise mentors of virtue? John would have his people attend to the Apostle Paul in preparation for finding a spouse. While one should "take great care to choose a wife who is well-ordered from the beginning and compatible with our character," (91) still the model is to love one's spouse "as Christ loved the Church" (Eph. 5.25). Referring to the Epistle to the Ephesians, John notes that Christ loved the church with gentleness and reformed it. So also is the nature of Christian marriage. Marriage is where we may become as Christ is; and, so, we will be formed in Christ-like virtue. Marriage is not about money or about gaining a worldly advantage, as seemed to be the case in John's city. Rather marriage is, according to Chrysostom, "a fellowship for life" (96). What riches should be sought for in such a fellowship for life? John's answer is that we seek one thing: "virtue of soul and nobility of character" (97).

One virtue seems to sum up marriage for John Chrysostom. That virtue is chastity. Chastity is, however, not mere sexual abstinence, but, rather, an orientation or appetite in all things for holiness. Whether we are celibates or are married, according to Chrysostom, "let us pursue holiness" (42). Christian holiness is, according to Chrysostom, "the gift of marriage, this is its fruit, this is its profit" (99). Chastity, as the pursuit of holiness, is "to be freed from all immorality" (99). This is what holds a Christian husband and wife together. Chrysostom describes this unity as more powerful than a union in body. It is a genuine friendship in virtue.

Chrysostom narrates the story of Abraham and Sarah to describe marriage as it ought to be, i.e., according to appropriate virtue or excellence. He notes that the virtue of the righteous Abraham is that he sought for his own son not "a rich or beautiful wife, but one who would be noble in her character" (101). When Abraham's servant, sent to look for a wife for Isaac, looks for a sign that this is the woman, he does not look for riches or beauty. The servant must find a woman of virtue, but what is the sign? The sign, according to Chrysostom, is generosity. Chrysostom claims that in Rebecca "virtue appears not only in what she did but in her willingness in doing it" (107–108). Rebecca is revealed to be like the family of Abraham, i.e., those who entertain messengers unaware. Importantly, Chrysostom demands that his listeners do "not listen to this as if it were an unimportant matter" (109). The purpose of the narrative is, according to Chrysostom, so that we might "consider ourselves and compare ourselves to these people" (109). "I have told this story," Chrysostom insists, "not only for you to hear, not only for you to praise, but also for you to emulate" (113).

The biblical narrative is also employed to describe the way of Christian virtue as it is reflected in the practice of the wedding celebration. Chrysostom suggests that Christians should celebrate their "weddings with as much decorum as Isaac did" (113). While marriage is undefiled and a way to gain the virtues characteristic of God, Chrysostom observes that in his community Christians "give marriage a bad name with depraved celebrations" (76 [*Colosians*, homily 12]). It is clear that for John Chrysostom what and why we celebrate is essential to gaining Christian virtue. Chrysostom wants to reform local wedding celebrations because local practices disguise what is God's gift in marriage. While Chrysostom describes marriage as an image of the presence of Christ, he finds his people becoming more skilled at imaging evil. Chrysostom asks his people if it is "not possible for pleasure and temperance to co-exist?" (78). If his people want songs, then sing those that contribute to our virtue. "Instead of dancing girls," pleads Chrysostom, "invite the choir of angels to your wedding" (78). These practices, according to Chrysostom in an obvious allusion to Scripture, are active in transforming us either from water to wine or from evil to worse.

"There is nothing," Chrysostom maintains, "more pleasurable than virtue" (78). Even the wedding celebration develops or disrupts the taste for virtue. Chrysostom reminds his congregation that "a wedding is not a pageant or a theatrical performance" (79). He claims that one should "invite as many people as you know to have good character" (79). These will share and nourish a friendship in Christ with you. Chrysostom next advises that the poor be invited to share the feast. "Think of the many good things," Chrysostom exhorts, "that will result from weddings like this!" (79). Chrysostom's conclusion is that when Christ is present at a wedding celebration, then Christian virtues are celebrated and, thereby, gained.

Sexuality also plays an ordering function—albeit minor—in the acquisition of Christian virtue according to John Chrysostom. He maintains that one who withholds conjugal relations from a spouse out of concern for purity has only "missed the mark." Such a practice is, according to Chrysostom, "a sin which outweighs the righteousness of their abstinence" (28 [*First Corinthians,* homily 19]). While Christian devotions might require a couple to forgo sexual relations, Chrysostom insists that this is not a matter of making prayer or the one praying unclean. Christians may abstain from sexual relations to pray because, practically, one cannot do both. "They occupy one's attention" (28). So to abstain from sexual relations is a practical matter that allows time for prayer, while to insist that it is done so as to remain above what is unclean is to mutilate virtue. The only difference between a monk and a lay Christian, according to Chrysostom, is that one has a spouse and the other does not. Chrysostom holds that when we compare a monk and a lay person, both of whom have committed adultery, it is the monk who should be more readily forgiven. "Indeed," Chrysostom explains, "the misdeed is not the same when someone who has a wife, and therefore enjoys consolation, is carried away by a woman's beauty; and when someone who is totally deprived of this is fettered by this evil." [36]

The same reasoning as is noted above may be found in Chrysostom's treatment of sexuality and the unbelieving spouse. "An unbelieving husband is impure," Chrysostom cautions, "because of his unbelief; but if his believing wife is not united to him in the act of unbelief, she remains pure." [37] Whatever one's situation—including that of being the unbelieving spouse—virtue is the goal. In a pastoral aside Chrysostom notes that "no teacher is so effective as a persuasive wife" (33).

In summary, to have a spouse is good. It can be a way to guide Christians, especially men it would seem, "to the practice of self control" (26). Self control here seems to mean the *giving* of conjugal rights. In this way Christians learn through the practice of marriage that "neither husband nor wife is his or her own master, but rather each other's servants" (26). To yield to one another is to gain the Christlike virtues of obedience and love, according to Chrysostom. "This, then, is what it means to marry in Christ: spiritual marriage is like spiritual birth" (54 [*Ephesians*, homily 20]). However, even the most spiritual spousal search, wedding, and marriage may result in children. What has virtue to do with children according to John Chrysostom?

In homily 21 on Ephesians 6.1–4, Chrysostom observes that the commandment to "honor your father and mother" is the first commandment to contain a promise, i.e., "that it may be well with you and that you may live long." He maintains that Paul employs the commandment in this way to properly order children. Paul "will not speak here about Christ, or other lofty subjects," according to Chrysostom, "but will direct his words to young minds" (65). According to Chrysostom, we should understand Paul's words as seeking a firm foundation for a life of virtue for children. The firm foundation to a life of virtue is to learn how to render honor and respect. "This is the first good practice, commanded us in the Scriptures," Chrysostom holds, "because before all others, except God, our parents are the authors of our life" (66). Chrysostom's ordering of virtue includes the claim that if you cannot learn to honor your parents, then you cannot expect to grow in any other virtue. "If a man does not honor his parents," Chrysostom claims, "he will never treat other people with kindness" (66).

Granted the establishment of honor in respect—which must be cultivated by parents' not tempting their children—how is a parent to nurture further growth in virtue? Chrysostom claims that next in importance are the stories that we tell. The primary collection of child-appropriate Christian narrative is the Bible. Chrysostom assures parents that to tell the scriptural stories to a child is not to try to make the child into a monk, but it is to "make him into a Christian!" (67). "Don't think," Chrysostom warns, "that it isn't necessary for a child to listen to the Scriptures" (67). "Even at their age they are exposed to all sorts of folly and bad examples from popular entertainments" (67). Chrysostom appeals to parents to see that not only monks need to learn the Bible; children about to go out into the world stand in greater need of scriptural knowledge. A man who never travels by sea doesn't need to know how to equip a ship, or where to find a pilot or a crew, but a sailor has to know these things (69).

Chrysostom claims, clearly, that patterns of life to imitate are a necessary element of the life of virtue. Virtue is what everyone, including children, really needs. In a passage rich with overtones of classical education, Chrysostom warns that a child

will not suffer if he lacks clever words; but if he lacks wisdom, all the rhetoric in the world can't help him. A pattern of life is what is needed, not empty speeches; character, not cleverness (69).

The figures of the Old Testament are offered by Chrysostom as the appropriate exemplars of virtue for children. "Would you like me," Chrysostom asks, "to give examples of men whose lives were patterns of virtue, even though they lived in the world?" (69). Chrysostom suggests Noah, Joseph, Moses, and Isaiah, but settles on Abraham. Abraham, Chrysostom observes, was not a monk but was married and had children. Why is Abraham an appropriate exemplar for Christian children? "Because of his hospitality, his detachment from riches, and his well-ordered life" (70). Chrysostom maintains that when we order our children to the characteristics of godlike hospitality, then we rightly equip them to navigate life. "Don't surround them," Chrysostom cautions,

with the external safeguards of wealth and fame, for when these fail—and they will fail—our children will stand naked and defenseless, having gained no profit from their former prosperity, but only injury, since when those artificial protections that shielded them from the winds are removed, they will be blown to the ground in a moment (71).

Wealth of the sort that most parents want for their children is not an attribute of God. Parents are, according to Chrysostom, like artists who work at revealing what is good and beautiful according to virtue. Parents are worthy artists when they order their family to reveal the image of God in themselves and in their children. "When we teach our children to be good, to be gentle, to be forgiving (all these are attributes of God), to be generous, to love their fellow men, to regard this present age as nothing," Chrysostom insists, "we instill virtue in their souls, and reveal the image of God within them" (71).

Chrysostom ends his sermon by asserting that "one's own virtue is not enough" (72). No, according to Chrysostom: "the virtue of those for whom we are responsible is also required" (72). Marriage and children has become for Chrysostom an ecclesial entity where in loving as God in Christ loved us, we can gain the virtue of Christ and so be saved.

SUMMARY

We may conclude that for the aforementioned Fathers the acquisition of virtue is of central and fundamental concern. For Athanasius, virtue is indispensable. Virtue, here understood as "skillfulness," is absolutely necessary in understanding the narratives of creation and redemption, i.e., the Bible. Virtue or the question of being cannot be separated from the problem of truth in Athanasius. Excellence in the way of truth is required if truth is to be recognized.

Virtue is then indispensable, and it is attained by practicing its ways. The practice of imitating the exemplars of the faith is fundamental to the acquisition of Christian virtue. Imitation of the Christian way of life is, evidently, even more fundamental than words of direction. Transformation by way of the imitation of the mentor's life of virtue may result in communion, in a sharing of vision. The skilled sharing of a vision of life's true end is the acquisition of Christian community. It is to have attained life.

The community gained is, then, a "fellowship of life." Attaining this fellowship is nothing less than communion in Christ. Christ is the true virtue or excellence of humanity. Sharing God's life, granted in love, is the end of human being. All attempts at "virtue" are limited by any separation from true life in God. The pursuit of human excellence outside of Christ is, therefore, always frustrated to some degree. Without God Incarnate, we do not know our true end; and all "practices" outside of the knowledge of God are products of narratives that are either blind or limited. The life in Christ is true virtue. Church is the community that understands the narratives of salvation and the practices of authentic virtue. The saints are mentors because they are Christ-bearers. "Aretology" permeates every aspect of the theology of Athanasius.

In the Cappadocians we find a virtue ethic that dares to stand face to face with classical modes. The Cappadocians challenge a society steeped in virtue to account for itself by its own standards. While the Cappadocians claim that Christianity is the source of true virtue, they also critique Christianity in terms of its claim to superior *paideia*. The Cappadocians agree with classical antiquity that life has an end, and that there are virtues to be acquired by an appropriate *paideia*. They assay themselves, their friends, their church, and their times, all in terms of virtue.

In John Chrysostom we find a mentor who envisages the family as the locus for making virtuous people for the community of the church. If family is about something other than the making of virtuous people, then it has no lasting foundation. A marriage is meaningful only if it is a union for, of, and by virtue. Family is an ecclesial practice where the transformative power of the Bible, the Christian narrative, is actualized to form a people of Christian virtue. In Chrysostom we discover that all are equally called to the contest of virtue.

The centrality of virtue might easily be illustrated by reference to other Patristic figures, but a somewhat fuller account of virtue is needed. *The Ladder of Divine Ascent* by John Climacus will serve that need. In John Climacus we find a mentor experienced in and able to show how a practice leads to a habit, and how habituation may take root like a second nature. John Climacus will trace the "ladder" of virtue that leads to God's love, and he will also describe a ladder of passions that leads to human destruction.

NOTES

1. Stanley Harakas, "Ethics in the Greek Orthodox Tradition," *The Greek Orthodox Theological Review* 22 (Spring 1977): 58–62, at 58.
2. Ibid.
3. Ibid.
4. The Cappadocian Fathers are Basil the Great, his younger brother Gregory of Nyssa, and their friend and fellow bishop Gregory of Nazianzus.
5. Johannes Quasten, *Patrology*, vol. 3, *The Golden Age of Greek Patristic Literature* (Westminster, Maryland: Christian Classics, Inc., 1984), 20.
6. Ibid.
7. Ibid.
8. *Contra Gentes and De Incarnatione*, trans./ed. Robert W. Thomson (Oxford: Clarendon Press, 1971), 269 (*De Incarnatione* 54).
9. Ibid., 153 (*De Incarnatione* 8).
10. Ibid., 173 (*De Incarnatione* 16).
11. Athanasius, *The Life of Anthony* and *The Letter to Marcellinus*, trans. Robert C. Gregg, *The Classics of Western Spirituality: A Library of the Great Spiritual Masters* (New York: Paulist Press, 1980), 112 (*Epistula ad Marcellinum de interpretatione Psalmorum* 13).
12. Ibid.
13. To the present day, the Psalms form the major portion of corporate daily worship in the Eastern Church. The hours (first, third, sixth, and ninth), vespers, matins, and compline are never employed as a private devotion for the cleric in the Christian East.

14. The awkwardness of this way of describing the function of music stems, no doubt, from the contemporary assumption that music is but a personal expression, a way of emoting. Music understood as a sort of practice that forms will reappear in Basil's "Address to Young Men on Reading Greek Literature," treated in the next section.

15. *Letter to Marcellinus*, 124 (28).

16. It is common to find in Patristic literature the claim that the human person is the truest instrument with which to praise God. Also common was the notion that one is moral when one becomes a "symphony" to God's creative fiat by being "played" by the Holy Spirit. It is surely correct that for the Eastern Church "music was a way of involving the whole self" in loving God. Everett Ferguson, "Toward a Patristic Theology of Music," *Studia Patristica* 24 (1993): 266–283.

17. *Letter to Marcellinus*, 129 (33).

18. *Life of Anthony*, 99 (*Vita Antonii* 93).

19. Ellen T. Charry, "The Case for Concern: Athanasian Christology in Pastoral Perspective," *Modern Theology* 9 (July 1993): 265–283, at 266.

20. Ibid., 267.

21. *Against Arians*, 3.19, quoted ibid., 274.

22. *Patrology*, vol. 3, 203.

23. Ibid.

24. *Epigram 7*, quoted in *Saint Gregory Nazianzen: Selected Poems*, trans. John McGucken (Oxford: Fairacres Publications, 1989), 19.

25. Gregory of Nyssa, *Life of Moses*, trans. Abraham J. Malherbe and Everett Ferguson, *The Classics of Western Spirituality: A Library of the Great Spiritual Masters* (New York: Paulist Press, 1978), 31 (*De vita Moysis* 1.7).

26. *Funeral Orations by Saint Gregory Nazianzen and Saint Ambrose*, trans. Leo P. McCauley and Roy J. Deferrari, *The Fathers of the Church* (New York: Fathers of the Church, Inc., 1953), 33.

27. Ibid., 30.

28. Ibid., 27–28.

29. Jaroslav Pelikan, *Christianity and Classical Culture* (New Haven : Yale University Press, 1993), 9.

30. Basil the Great, *The Letters*, vol.4, trans. Roy J. Deferrari, Loeb Classical Library, ed. E.H. Warmington, no. 270 (Cambridge: Harvard University Press, 1970), 381 (*Ad adolescentes*, sect. 1).

31. Pelikan, *Christianity*, 157.

32. Quasten, *Patrology*, vol. 3, 424.

33. Ibid.

34. Ibid., 429.

35. John Chrysostom, *On Marriage and Family Life*, trans./ed. Catharine P. Roth and David Anderson, with an introduction by Catharine P. Roth (Crestwood, New York: St. Vladimir's Seminary Press, 1986), 7.

36. *Adversus oppugnatores vitae monasticae*, 3. 15, Irènèe Hausherr, *Spiritual Direction in the Early Christian East*, trans. Anthony P. Gythiel (Kalamazoo, Michigan: Cistercian Publications, 1990), 308.

37. John Chrysostom, *On Marriage*, 32 (*First Corinthians*, homily 19).

3

The Pursuit of Virtue in The Ladder of Divine Ascent

The purpose of this chapter is to locate and define virtue in the Orthodox Church more specifically than was offered in the previous chapter, which was intended primarily to defend the claim of the general importance of virtue for the Greek Fathers. This chapter's move toward greater specificity in the understanding of virtue in the Greek Church will be accomplished by presenting an account of virtue as it is found in *The Ladder of Divine Ascent* by John Climacus. The six formal elements of *telos*, practice, virtue, community, narrative, and mentoring will continue to guide and orient the inquiry, but the chapter will follow the order of presentation found in *The Ladder*. It is important to John Climacus that he show that the virtues are not arbitrary and that they require a particular order and unity. For that reason, my inquiry will not stray far from the given text. At the very end of his work (step 30), he writes: "Let this ladder teach you the spiritual union of the virtues." [1] (All references to John Climacus: *The Ladder* are quoted from the Luibheid/ Russell translation except where otherwise noted.) I will, however, focus his presentation to illumine the concepts of virtue, passions, the spiritual father as mentor, the *telos* of love, and narrative.

The Ladder of Divine Ascent was selected for two reasons. First, according to the Introduction to *The Ladder* by the well-known authority and bishop, Timothy Ware, "with the exception of the Bible and the service books, there is no work in Eastern Christendom that has been studied, copied and translated more than *The Ladder of Divine Ascent* by St. John Climacus." [2] Second, *The Ladder* was selected because "by far the larger part of the work is concerned with the practice of the virtues." [3] The importance of virtue in the Greek Church tradition seems to be borne out by *The Ladder*, inasmuch as this most popular work after the Bible is, as noted, primarily a book about the acquisition of virtue. However, the text has never been used as a source specifically to shape ethics. It has been treated, primarily, as pious spiritual reading for the monastic refectory.

Ware writes that "John's basic image, around which the entire book is structured, is a ladder stretching from earth to heaven like that which Jacob saw (Gen. 28.12)." [4] While the image of a ladder is to be found elsewhere in Patristic literature, John Climacus developed it more than anyone before or after him. In his hands, the ladder seen by Jacob is transformed into a way of climbing toward God. Each of the thirty steps of the ladder stand for a year in the life of Jesus before his baptism, the time of his maturation.

The Ladder is, it would seem, an expression of "typological" interpretation of the Scriptures. "Typology" is understood to be the basic mode by which Orthodox Christians interpret the Scriptures. "A 'type' (*typos*) may be defined as a prophetic image (a person, place, object, or event) that points forward to and is fulfilled by a corresponding future reality (the antitype)." [5] Typological interpretation as employed by Orthodox Christianity is profoundly teleological, and involves the claim that the Scripture—indeed, *everything*—is fulfilled in Christ.

Orthodox Christians understand Adam as having turned from God who is life and so brought death into the world; the New Adam, Christ, never turned from the Father and, so, in him we find the life that was lost. Adam is a "type" fulfilled in Christ. So too, as Moses led the people of Israel out of captivity, Moses' "type" is fulfilled in the antitype of Christ who leads his people, the Church, to the Kingdom. In the case of the primary imagery of *The Ladder*, the way through the desert, the ladder itself, and Jacob, are all fulfilled in Christ. It is clear at this point that Christ serves for John Climacus as the paradigm for virtuous humanity. Typological interpretation may be seen as the discerning of links between "figures" and their completion as uncovered by their end. It is the "deep grammar" of the text as read by Orthodox Christians. The Scriptures are understood as meaningful in their being fulfilled, just as humanity is "understood" as being fulfilled in the *telos* of Christ. Orthodox Christianity, it would seem, is essentially teleological in its interpretive orientation.

Both the desert experience of the Hebrew Scriptures and Greek *paideia* find their completion in Christ. While *The Ladder* is, indeed, an expression of Christian typology, it is, not so obviously, also a rival account of virtue in classical form. While the text employs scriptural figures, John Climacus also displays a traditional Greek virtue ethic as transformed by a Christian *telos*, with Christian practices and Christian virtues completing the Greek counterparts. Where Aristotle's ethics describes the virtue of the citizen of the Greek polis, in which courage is a central and necessary human excellence, John Climacus describes the virtue of a Christian who must be transformed not by courage, but by the virtue of repentance in order to gain citizenship in the New Jerusalem.

Contemporary virtue ethicists have been accused of being too optimistic about the human condition and the possibility of virtue. James Chansky has claimed that theorists like MacIntyre are too quick in their rejection of pessimism. He claims that such ethics "tend for the most part to view evil as playing no positive role in either morals or morality, as at best a sad commentary but never an intrinsic part of the drama itself." [6] Climacus can never be accused of being thus flawed, and his ladder will be shown to have an important place for passions and vices in the acquisition of true virtue. Indeed, it has been noted that even the passions in *The Ladder* have a typological structure. [7] Carnal passions are described by John as a "*typos*" to be fulfilled—and transformed—by divine love. On the very last rung of the ladder, we read that fortunate is the one "who loves and longs for God as a smitten lover does for his beloved." [8]

STEPS OF VIRTUE

Just as Aristotle's work begins by establishing the many "goods" and then the one good of life, *eudaimonia,* [9] and continues by establishing the practices and virtues that allow for gaining the good life, so *The Ladder* begins by locating God as the supreme good for humanity, and continues by describing the virtues that are necessary to move toward that end. A *telos* or goal must be established, according to John Climacus, because "a blind archer is useless." [10] All of humankind are like archers, and life is our mark. "God is the life," he claims, "of all free beings" (74 [step 1]). This is the supreme good for all humanity, i.e., to live the life found only in God.

The path to the virtues found in Christ must first lead us from out of captivity to every inadequate *telos.* "Those of us who wish to get away from Egypt, to escape from Pharaoh," writes John Climacus, "need some Moses" (75). Jesus is our "Moses," come to lead us to freedom. Those who participate in the new life that the New Adam brings are, like Christ, called to be mentors of the way to life. It is a basic deception to think that one can do without a mentor. "Those who have given themselves up to God, but imagine that they can go forward without a leader are surely deceiving themselves" (75). It is painful to turn from the idols of life that we have constructed, and "we must travel through overwhelming grief toward the love of God and holiness" (75).

The first seven steps [11] are concerned with the difficult work of reorienting ourselves from any *telos* that is not God. These steps are renunciation, detachment, exile, obedience, penitence, remembrance of death, and mourning. They will dig the foundations of a life in Christ, the true virtue of humanity. "Some people," John Climacus observes, "when they build a house place bricks on top of rocks." [12] If we are to build a sturdy foundation for the virtues, then we must first learn to reject anything not of God. Movement through the first seven steps is primarily a journey of detachment from the world. This arduous progression will result either in acquired meekness or in its opposite, anger.

"At the beginning of our religious life," he cautions, "we cultivate the virtues, and we do so with toil and difficulty" (77). The difficulty is one of reordering our loves. John observes:

> We should love the Lord as we do our friends. Many a time I have seen people bring grief to God, without being bothered about it, and I have seen these very same people resort to every device, plan, pressure, plea from themselves and their friends, and every gift, simply to restore an old relationship upset by some minor grievance (77).

If we are to restore friendship with God, we must acquire meekness. Meekness is the overcoming of any presumptuousness. Meekness is also necessary if we are to be mentored by a spiritual father. "John is emphatic," according to Timothy Ware, "about the importance of the spiritual father" (36). Without meekness, Christ would not have done the will of the Father. Without meekness, one will not follow a mentor. John Climacus cautions that however wise in the ways of the world, one "may easily go astray on a road if he has no guide" (259). Without meekness we can neither follow a mentor, nor find God.

Meekness is established in a community. John Climacus claims that the words from The Wisdom of Solomon 3.6, that "the Lord has tried them in a furnace," means "in a community" (120). A community is like a furnace where the gold of virtue is produced. Those who seek to renounce (step 1) every good that is not the good of God will need to find detachment (step 2), exile (step 3), and obedience (step 4) in a properly ordered community. Only in such a community can the vices—which are, as it were, spurious virtues—be uprooted. He explains in step 2:

> I have seen many different plants of the virtues planted by them in the world, watered by vanity as if from an underground cesspool, made to

shoot up by love of show, manured by praise, and yet they quickly withered when transplanted to desert soil, to where the world did not walk, that is, to where they were not manured with the foul-smelling water of vanity. The things that grow in water cannot bear fruit in dry and arid places (82).

A community ordered to the *telos* of God's life as found in Christ is, then, a place where the practices of inappropriate self-love will find no nourishment. In such a community one will only find exile from whatever "hinders one from attaining the ideal of holiness" (85). He describes the practice of exile as "the striving to be humble, a wish for poverty, the longing for what is divine" (85). This step on the ladder results in one becoming an exile to the world. Such a one is "like someone of foreign speech among men of other tongues" (87). He continues to develop the idea of exile by saying, "As flower comes before every fruit, so exile . . . precedes all obedience" (91).

Obedience to a community and a mentor results in the practical realization that one is not the source and end of one's life but is created in the image of God. "Obedience is self-mistrust up to one's dying day, in every matter, even the good" (92). Expanding on step 4, he writes:

Obedience is a total renunciation of our own life, and it shows up clearly in the way we act. Or, again, obedience is the mortification of the members while the mind remains alive. Obedience is unquestioned movement, death freely accepted, a simple life, danger faced without worry, an unprepared defense before God, fearlessness before death, a safe voyage, a sleeper's journey. Obedience is the burial place of the will and the resurrection of lowliness. A corpse does not contradict or debate the good or whatever seems bad, and the spiritual father who has devoutly put the disciple's soul to death will answer for everything (91–92).

Thus far John's *Ladder* has established that God is the true good of life. If one is to acquire the virtues of such a life, then one must practice the renunciation of any other *telos*. The turning toward God as life's *telos* shows itself in a change of practices, in a mortifying of all desires but the desire for God. It is an embracing of self-death in order to awaken to the resurrection of faith in God. Discernment at this level is the awareness that without God who is life, one is dead, a corpse. Such a one has need of a mentor and a community in order to make progress. After obedience comes penitence (step 5), remembrance of death (step 6), and mourning (step 7). It is in these three positive or developmental steps that narrative begins to gain importance. Prior to this level, one is unable to entertain the Christian narrative, because that story requires the rejection of the self and the recognition of God as one's end.

Penitence, remembrance of death, and mourning are all practices that develop obedience into a higher form of discernment called meekness. This part of the ladder is built around a narrative of repentance introduced at the very beginning of step 5. "Come, gather round, listen here and I will speak," John Climacus announces, "to all of you who have angered the Lord" (121). What follows is "the story of the dishonored workers—who still earned respect" (121). He claims to have visited a special monastery called "The Prison." Here he found an "abode of penitents" and a "place of true grief." In this "place" the monks wept, cried, and sorrowed over having fallen from the heights of true virtue. He describes for many pages what ought to be an awful place filled with terrible people, but in the middle of the story he begins to observe that here there was no anger, vanity, or quarreling among them. Without fail they encouraged one another. Instead of despair, he found a community of humility and love. He claims, "I came close to despair when I had seen and heard all this among them and when I had compared my own indifference with what they went through" (127). John claims to have remained for what is certainly a symbolic thirty days. He tells his reader that before leaving he spoke to the wise superior of that place. When asked what he saw, John Climacus responds that with amazement "it seems to me that those who have fallen and are penitent are more blessed than those who have never fallen and who do not have to mourn over themselves, because through having fallen, they have pulled themselves up by a sure resurrection" (128).

The narrative is undoubtedly intended to display a sort of "hero." The hero of this story exhibits the virtue of repentance. For John Climacus, repentance functions like courage or endurance might for the hero of classical Greek narratives. [13] In order to continue toward one's *telos*, the classical hero has need of courage, but for the initiate on the way that John Climacus is describing, one needs to be able to repent time and again with the awareness that such repeated repentance leads somewhere.

John Climacus encourages repentance; but to despair, its excess, is "to inflict death on oneself." [14] "Note well," he observes, "that we never return by the road on which we strayed, but rather by a different and a shorter route" (131). This step (5) is concluded with the observation that repentance is the way by which we purify ourselves by choosing a voluntary death in place of an involuntary death, that would be the result of living a life not grounded in God. The narrative of "The Prison" invites the hearer to imaginatively transform the notion of sin and failure from one of despair to one of increasing competence on the hard path of virtue. All learners make mistakes, even those learning holiness. The narrative supplied by this community functions to reveal the grammar of faith as one that parses sin with hope.

To maintain and feed the awareness that we are not our own end, John Climacus prescribes the remembrance of death (step 6). He maintains that

> just as bread is the most necessary of all foods, so the thought of death is the most essential of all works. The remembrance of death brings labors and meditations, or rather, the sweetness of dishonor to those living in community, whereas for those living away from turbulence it produces freedom from daily worries and breeds constant prayer and guarding the mind, virtues that are the cause and the effect of the thought of death (132).

The "remembrance of death," then, is also transformed by way of a narrative. Remembering that one will die brings freedom and, so, contributes to nourishing virtue as life in Christ.

It is clear that John Climacus is not encouraging some sort of suicidal intent. He writes that "not every desire for death is good. A habitual sinner prays humbly for death, but the man who does not want to change his ways may, in sheer despair, actually long for death" (133). The remembrance of death as a step on the ladder of true virtue is a way to become free from all that is not essential, free to be changed. This section is concluded with the observation that "even the Greeks have said some such thing, because they describe philosophy as meditation on death" (135).

Mourning (step 7) is an extension of the last two steps. John Climacus describes this as a disposition of the heart that "passionately seeks what it thirsts for, and when it fails to attain it, pursues it diligently" (136). Not to continue the turn to God would be, according to him, to "imitate those who in burying the dead first lament them—and then go off to get drunk" (138). He encourages those who hear him to cultivate mourning, which is "the beauty of your lowliness" (143).

Without meekness (step 8), the next steps on virtue's way cannot be attempted. Anger is the absence of, even the antithesis of meekness. [15] "Angry people," he claims, "because of their self-esteem, make a pitiable sight though they do not realize this themselves." [16] A short and memorable narrative functions to unify his contrast of meekness and anger. He writes that

> while engaged on some task, I happened to be sitting outside a monastery and near the cells of those living in solitude. I could overhear them

raging alone in their cells and in their bitter fury leaping about like caged partridges, leaping at the face of their offender as if he were actually there. My humble advice to them was to abandon solitary living in case they be turned from human beings into devils. [17]

At the end of step 8, John Climacus makes clear that this formation is of no little importance. It is not enough simply to be meek and avoid anger. One may be meek out of a certain natural disposition to avoid conflict, but such a person has not gained the requisite skill to continue to climb. We read that

on the eighth step the crown is freedom from anger. He who wears it by nature may never come to wear another. But he who has sweated for it and won it has conquered all eight together. [18]

Having conquered the first eight steps and having arrived at a certain degree of meekness and discernment, the seeker after virtue may now continue to progress. The ascent from meekness understood as the summit of the first eight steps, to meekness purified into true humility (step 25) involves a long and arduous passage where vice and virtue often intertwine in the tangle of the human heart. The large central portion of *The Ladder*, still to be traversed, reflects the complexity of the human person. That section of *The Ladder* is revelatory of the very life of virtue: It is not so easily mapped and progress is not simply upward. God is encountered there in moments of revelation as the one who both destroys and who also lifts up.

Meekness at this juncture—the culmination of the first eight steps, but only the beginning of the next level—is the virtue whereby one has just begun to discern that God is one's only good or *telos*. Only God can give life, and the practice of the awareness of death has made possible the renunciation of all that is not God. In so doing, one begins to detach oneself from the practices of self-love and becomes an exile from the world. Progress toward true obedience is now possible, and one is now able to continue in a community of mentors. Community narratives have fostered skill at repenting, and the remembrance of death and mourning have sustained progress toward meekness. While meekness is the summit of the first stage, it is not yet true humility because humility is grounded in love. Meekness is still rooted in either fear or reward. There is still an element of "self-as-*telos*" as long as fear or reward remain. God is love, not fear. The next steps on the ladder are where the remnants of self-love may be exorcized. [19]

John Climacus ends the section on meekness by returning to the dangers of anger. Meekness and anger have similar structures. One is ordered to God; the other to self. Anger, therefore, is a sure sign of presumptuousness. Someone in need of their very life is not presumptuous. "Fever suffered by the body," he observes, "is a single symptom but has many causes." [20] So it is with anger, which also has many causes. The movement from step 9 through step 23 involves the struggle from malice to pride. This is an attempt to use what has been learned on the ladder to bring the many causes of anger—which prevent one from gaining the virtue of humility, or meekness purified—"before the tribunal of reason" (150). The "choice" at the eighth step was between anger or meekness. One may go either way. Meekness leads to life as its end, while anger's end is death.

Giving voice to the vices and virtues, John Climacus asks anger to "tell us the name of your father, the name of your mother who bore you to bring calamity into the world, the names of your loathsome sons and daughters" (150). Anger answers that among his relatives are pride, avarice, greed, conceit, hostility, and self-justification. Anger continues to speak by naming its enemy "who has the power to kill" (150). Anger tells him that "the enemies who have imprisoned me are the opposite virtues—Freedom from Anger and Lowliness, while Humility lays a trap for me" (151). The pursuit of the virtue of humility will, then, destroy all of the vices that come between us and our *telos*.

The vices, born of anger and borne by presumptuousness, are dissembled and exposed as "still-born" at the next level of the ladder in the light of the discernment gained by practicing meekness. At the beginning of the step (9) concerning malice, John Climacus again presents the pursuit of virtue as a choice between life and death, freedom for and frustration of life's end. He writes that

> the holy virtues are like the ladder of Jacob and the unholy vices are like the chains that fell off the chief apostle Peter. The virtues lead from one to another and carry heavenward the man who chooses them. Vices on the other hand beget and stifle one another (152).

Malice is, therefore, unlike virtue in that "it comes to be but has no offspring" (152). It is "the ruin of virtues, the poison of the soul, a worm in the mind" (152). It is an absence of love that nourishes malice. John Climacus asks how one can both remember Jesus and remember wrongs done to us? "The remembrance of what Jesus suffered," he claims, "is a cure for remembrance of wrongs, shaming it powerfully with His patient endurance" (154). But if we are not yet able to renounce malice and grasp love because of the God who is love and our end, then, he advises, "go to your enemy and apologize, if only with empty words whose insincerity may shame you" (153). Here the necessary order and logic of the virtues, according to John Climacus, are uncovered. To banish anger and malice is more fundamental than forgiveness. Forgiveness is impossible as long as one labors under the illusions forged by anger. He writes that

> some labor and struggle hard to earn forgiveness, but better than these is the man who forgets the wrongs done to him. Forgive quickly and you will be abundantly forgiven. To forget wrongs is to prove oneself truly repentant, but to brood on them and at the same time to imagine one is practicing penitence is to act like the man who is convinced he is running when in fact he is fast asleep (154).

Slander, step 10, is an extension of malice. John Climacus notes sagely that he has spoken to people actually engaged in slander, a form of *self-defense*, who claimed to be acting out of love. He writes that his answer to such as these was to say: "stop that kind of love" (155). He seems to see the one acting in this way as confusing and obscuring the *telos* of life. If "slander" is a sort of "discernment," then this is not the sort taught by the Psalms. He quotes Psalm 63.7: "They have searched out iniquity and died in the search." Slander is, according to John Climacus, a "habit of passing judgment" (157). Such a practice would be effective only in moving one toward a *telos* of self-love. He is in search of what would nourish true virtue. He suggests that

> a good grape picker chooses to eat ripe grapes and does not pluck what is unripe. A charitable and sensible mind takes careful note of the virtues it observes in another, while the fool goes looking for faults and defects (157).

Talkativeness (step 11) is one of the practices that is a source of anger and the remembrance of wrongs. The tongue, John Climacus holds, is like the rest of a person; it, too, "needs to be trained in its habits" (158). Without the habit of silence, "the chatterer has yet to discover himself as he should" (159).

While talkativeness is a misapprehension of the self as its own end, falsehood (step 12) is the very denial of God. Those who lie, according to John Climacus, not only destroy the practice of living with God as *telos*, but also "have miserably destroyed in their hearers the habit of mourning" (159). The power of community is illustrated here because John Climacus sees great danger in our propensity not to contradict one who is witty. In so honoring them, we find it difficult not to be like them. The witty liar is a seductive sort of false mentor. The narrative world that the liar fashions displays a realm where we are the authors of what is, and then he bids us enter.

Despondency (step 13) is the tedium that comes to one in search of true virtue. In its wake follows gluttony (step 14), chastity (step 15), avarice (step 16), poverty (step 17), insensitivity (step 18), sleep (step 19), alertness (step 20), cowardice (step 21), vainglory (step 22), and pride (step 23). All are related inasmuch as they are all habits of life which lead to the apprehension—or misapprehension—of our *telos* and, thus, of true virtue. All of these, according to John Climacus, are, like gluttony, an insatiable habit to make of everything a "feast" for one's own ends. Gluttony is the antithesis of Eucharist. Eucharist is a feast of Christ for others. If gluttony is a "war against [our] bodies," then chastity is a battle for the spirit.

One who has become chaste "is not, someone with a body undefiled but rather a person whose members are in complete subjection to the soul, for a man is great who is free of passion even when touched, though greater still is the man unhurt by all that he has looked on" (172). John Climacus is again applauding the efficacy of the struggle for virtue. [21] He notes that

> some have praised those who are naturally eunuchs. They say of them that they have been freed from the martyrdom of the body. But as far as I am concerned my praise goes out each day to those who take the knife, so to speak, to their own evil thoughts. [22]

Avarice (step 16) is, according to John Climacus, "a worship of idols and is the offspring of unbelief" (187). If a person has practiced renunciation on the way to humility, then such a one is sure to be generous. To strive against avarice and for poverty (step 17) is described by John Climacus as a contest, an *agonia*. For the one who has given up the self as a final end, there can be neither avarice nor poverty. Accordingly, to acquire poverty or detachment is "to escape all the vices mentioned above" (190). Poverty is the fruit of practicing mourning over one's self as the source of life and of rejoicing in the riches of God.

Insensitivity (step 18) comes when negligence of virtue has become a habit. According to John Climacus:

> The insensitive man is a foolish philosopher, an exegete condemned by his own words, a scholar who contradicts himself, a blind man teaching

sight to others. He talks about healing a wound and does not stop making it worse. He complains about what has happened and does not stop eating what is harmful. He prays against it but carries on as before, doing it and being angry with himself. And the wretched man is in no way shamed by his own words. 'I'm doing wrong,' he cries, and zealously continues to do so. His lips pray against it and his body struggles for it. He talks profoundly about death and acts as if he will never die (191).

Sensitivity, in contrast, is where the ladder is properly to lead. To become aware of our true end is to become a "lover of wisdom," a true exegete and scholar of life, not blind to virtue's standard in God.

Turning the ladder on himself, John Climacus notes that insensitivity is something with which he is very familiar. Describing himself, he notes that failure here results in one who "teaches meekness and frequently gets angry while he is teaching" (192). The sources of this vice are many and varied, he observes, but time and bad habits will surely fix insensitivity in one's character, so as never to be rid of it. The next steps will correct the practice that leads to insensitivity by prescribing less sleep, and more prayer and psalmody, which leads to alertness and roots out the last vestiges of vainglory and pride.

Once more John Climacus is resorting to a classical understanding of habit. Habit is how one traditionally acquired virtue. [23] Virtue is an excellence that is peculiar to our being, to our being as revealed in Christ. Vice is, then, to become less than human by habit. "A long-standing habit," he maintains, "is very difficult to correct." [24] Sleep is understood by John Climacus to be a natural state, but "it is also an image of death and a respite of the senses" (194). It is clear that for John Climacus a person of true virtue is rising from the dead and gaining a sense of discernment. Sleep is not the image of a person of virtue. The image offered by him is that of a fit wrestler, awake and ready for the contest. Vigil is the opposite of slumber. It is life, awareness, and struggle.

Vigil, in contrast to sleep, becomes, among other things, a "net" for the mind, according to John Climacus, that catches what is required for true virtue. This is called alertness. Illustrating how vigil forms the mind to be alert to the things of God, he explains that

the farmer collects his wealth on the threshing floor and in the winepress. Monks collect their wealth and knowledge during the hours of evening and night when they are standing at prayer and contemplation (197).

Vigil is how one becomes aware and alert to what will give life. In contrasting alertness to God with insensitivity, John Climacus writes that

> the inexperienced monk is wide awake when talking to his friends but half asleep at prayer time. The lazy monk is a great talker whose eyes begin to shut when the sacred reading is started. When the trumpet sounds the dead will rise, and when idle talk begins the dozing wake (197).

For those who seek after true virtue, he promises, there will come times of fear. Fear comes to the one who still has preserved some remnant of the self as *telos*. "A proud soul is the slave of cowardice" (199). He concludes that this is so because "trusting only in itself, it is frightened by a sound or a shadow" (199). It is not enough to be free of fear—John Climacus notes that robbers are often fearless. Fearlessness is the discernment gained by practice that after God there is nothing to be feared. [25] "The servant of the Lord will be afraid only of his Master," John Climacus holds, "while the man who does not fear Him is often scared by his own shadow." [2]

Vainglory (step 22) and pride (step 23) complete the steps on the ladder between meekness and the summit of humility. Vainglory is but another form of self-esteem. It is, John Climacus claims, "from the point of view of form . . . a change of nature, a perversion of character" (201). It is the particular danger of one who has made progress in virtue, only to turn the progress into a narrative of self-worth. At this rung of the ladder one is able to withstand any offense, but is toppled by praise. John Climacus offers story after story to illustrate the logic of vainglory:

> The Lord frequently hides from us even the perfections we have obtained. But the man who praises us, or, rather, who misleads us, opens our eyes with his words and once our eyes are opened our treasures vanish (202).

Just as meekness can be established and then cultivated into humility, so vainglory can become pride. Life is a dynamic movement toward virtue or vice, as determined by our *telos* rightly or wrongly grasped, aided by the practices of a community, narratives, and mentors.

"Pride begins," John Climacus claims, "where vainglory leaves off" (207). It is a subtle denial of God. "It is a flight from God's help, the harbinger of madness, the author of downfall" (207). This, the crown of the vices, is as powerfully subtle as humility is strong. "Listen, therefore," warns John Climacus,

> all who wish to avoid this pit. This passion often draws strength initially from the giving of thanks, and at first it does not shamelessly urge us to renounce God. I have seen people who speak aloud their thanks to God but who in their hearts are glorifying themselves (207).

The proud person is still navigating in a world where he, and not God, is in charge. If the proud person is not in charge, "he would feel lost otherwise" (208). If there is always the danger of self-conceit in a virtue ethic, it is identified and countered in John's *Ladder*. He demands that

> while it is disgraceful to be puffed up over the adornments of others, it is sheer lunacy to imagine that one has deserved the gifts of God. You may be proud only of the achievements you had before the time of your birth. But anything after that, indeed the birth itself, is a gift from God. You may claim only those virtues in you that are there independently of your mind, for your mind was bestowed on you by God (209).

A person's true self, the self of virtue or excellence, is a gift from God, a grace; but every gift must be received. If the gift is life, then it must be chosen, entered, and lived. Because of this, according to John Climacus, "the proud never really discover their true selves" (210). Being proud, they are not skilled at receiving a gift.

Step 24 is a summary chapter. There is a necessary order to the virtues. "The true order of the virtues," John Climacus insists, "teaches us that we are totally unable to turn our eyes to the sun before we have first become accustomed to the light" (214). Only the meek can be taught God's ways (Ps 24.9). Meekness formed into true humility becomes a way of knowing, just as anger, according to John Climacus, is a kind of knowing. [27] Simplicity and guilelessness are characteristic of the sort of knowing that comes from meekness. This is true *theoria*, the perception of Divine Truth, of who we are and where we are called. For Orthodox Christians, epistemology would seem to be connected to virtue.

If you have come this far (step 24), he announces, "you are imitating Christ your Master and you have been saved." [28] Only those virtues whose intelligible context are God's grace are to be sought. He writes that good and blessed is that simplicity which some have by nature, but better is that which has been goaded out of wickedness by hard work. The former is protected from much complexity and the passions, while the latter is the gateway to the greatest humility and meekness. There is not much reward for the one and no end of reward for the other (216).

We have at this point reached the top most steps of the ladder of Christian virtue. We are now gathered together in the fellowship of life. "Let all who are led by the Spirit of God," John Climacus writes, "come with us into this spirited and wise assembly" (218). For those who have sought after true virtue and climbed the ladder, John Climacus can advise them to

hold in their spiritual hands the tablets of knowledge inscribed by God Himself. We have come together. We have put our questions. We have searched for the meaning of this precious inscription (218).

"Holy Humility," he declares, is what we will have found. The "queen of virtues" is humility. Humility (step 25) is the name that John Climacus gives to sharing the life that is found only in God. [29] He prescribes the practice of writing all of the virtues on one's wall and then to cry out: "When you have every one of these virtues within you, then you will have an accurate sense of how far from God you still are." [30] God is the *telos* that is never exhausted, but ever sought. Just as "there is no boundary to virtue," (250) so there is no limit to love. Humility, the queen of the virtues, is also the door to love. Growth in the virtue that is a gift of God's love will never cease, and, as with the angels, we may "add glory to glory and knowledge to knowledge" (251). Humility will foster growth in discernment (step 26), stillness (step 27), prayer (step 28), and dispassion (step 29), and, as noted, all in the direction of God's love (step 30).

"The sea is the source of the fountain and humility is the source of discernment" (228). Discernment is described by John Climacus as "knowing how the wind is blowing, [so that] we may set our sails accordingly" (230). With discernment one can now see the pitfalls to Christian virtue that waited all along the ladder from first to last. First, according to John Climacus, is the pitfall of making no attempt at all, not to strive. Second, is the pitfall of making "progress," but not in accord with the *telos* of God. These potential obstacles on the ladder are present all along the way and until our dying day, according to John Climacus. To discern all of this from high on the ladder is described as "pure perception" (229). "To put the matter generally, discernment is and is recognized to be—a solid understanding of the will of God in all times, in all places, and in all things; and it is found only among those who are pure in heart, in body, and in speech" (229). All of which is possible. "No one," he writes, "should plead inability to do what is asked of us in the gospels, since there are souls who have accomplished far more than is commanded" (231).

With growth in the virtue of discernment is to be found a certain maturity, stillness, or *hesychia* (step 27). *Hesychia* is defined in *The Ladder*

> as the *unceasing* worship of God. For the true hesychast, inward prayer is not so much an occasional occupation as a continuous state; it is not merely one activity among others, but *the* activity of his whole life (53).

It is the *peace* that comes with uniting what ought to be (God's will) with what is for me. *Hesychia* is the peace of the union of humanity and God. It is the peace of the recreation of creation. John calls this dialogue in virtue, prayer.

Prayer (step 28) is the dialogue of divine union, what "holds the world together" (272). If prayer holds the world together, it is clear that, for him, it also holds together the person of virtue. If you love virtue, then "enclose your mind with the words of your prayer" (276). But is the prayer of the hesychast an escape to otherworldly contemplation? It would seem that for John Climacus even in prayer and *hesychia* there is no escape from the struggle for virtue and its demands. Even at this level, he explains that one

> is examined each day without fail regarding what he has learned from his teacher. And it is reasonable to ask that there be a reckoning of each prayer we have undertaken, in order that we may have an idea of the power we have received from God. You should see to this. And when you have prayed soberly, you will soon have to cope with bouts of ill temper, something our enemies aim for (279).

The conclusion to the section on prayer prescribes—in common with the tradition of virtue reaching back to the ancient Greeks—that one learn to do by doing. "You cannot learn to see," John Climacus maintains, "just because someone tells you to do so" (281). You also cannot learn to pray without praying, and, at that, praying until the habit becomes, in time, one's virtue. John Climacus concludes:

> He grants prayer of him who prays. And He blesses the years of the just (281).

Dispassion [31] (step 29) is said by John to be nothing short of a resurrection. "Dispassion is resurrection of the soul prior to that of the body, while others would insist that it is a perfect knowledge of God, a knowledge second only to that of the angels." [32] "Dispassion is," as described by John Climacus, "an uncompleted perfection of the perfect" (282). Taking a stand on the ancient question of the unity of the virtues, John Climacus holds at this point that "just as a royal crown is not made up of one stone, so dispassion is incomplete if we neglect even one of the most ordinary virtues" (284).

If dispassion unites all of the virtues in a passage from death to resurrection—because it is the virtue of having turned from any inadequate passion—then love (step 30) makes us to sit "with the princes of God's people" (285). Love is the summit of the ladder of Christian virtues. [33] It is, according to John Climacus, "a resemblance to God, insofar as this is humanly possible." [34]

Summaries of his account of the acquisition of Christian virtue are provided all along the ladder. Reminiscent of Aristotle, John Climacus notes at one point that "as everyone knows there are differences of concept and aim in each of the sciences" (265). The measure of the science of virtue is, according to John, "a delight in, a thirst for the love and sweetness of God" (265). Unlike other "sciences," then, the science of virtue is eminently practical. It is the science that shows the ways of God.

Virtue is that excellence that can be acquired after every false end is rejected, which is a key to understanding at every level of *The Ladder*. Mentors, narratives, and community facilitate the practice of virtue. Without God the narrative of our lives takes on the tragic dimension of the story of pseudo-divinity. The ordering of life to a false *telos* necessarily makes lies of our stories and distorts our communities into becoming places where vice is nourished. Humanity, as free, cannot be compelled to find the love of God. Olivier Clément has amplified this idea:

> The gift of grace saves, but only in an encounter of love. Grace develops the individual, the whole person, like an atmosphere ready to seep in through the smallest breach. But only faith in its sovereign freedom can cause the breach to be made. Then it becomes an active opening-up, the beginning of abandonment to the divine life. And for the good of humanity as a whole some are 'set apart', for it is not the isolated individual but humanity in communion, or rather, in human beings together, who truly constitute the image of God. We can see that this 'complete Adam', this 'single man', is fragmented; we are continually breaking him in pieces. But Christ, the 'definitive Adam', puts him together again, the same but different, in the likeness of the Trinity. [35]

SUMMARY

According to *The Ladder*, virtue is gained with much effort over a long and dangerous ascetical journey. The journey is infinitely long because our virtue is God, and God's excellence is ever beyond our grasp. [36] It is, therefore, not simply the acquisition of virtue per se that drives such an ethic, because virtue is always in God who is beyond possession. Not virtue but eros, that is, God—love beyond possession—drives such an ethic.

Virtue in *The Ladder* is understood as coming naturally to humanity. [37] Yet, passion is described there as not simply something to be overcome, but as that which contributes positively to formation in virtue. In *The Ladder*, passion is "not an *act* of sin, a specific 'fall,' it is a *state* resulting from many specific acts of consent and falls." [38] Passion, if it is essentially sinful, would have only negative importance in *The Ladder*. John Climacus would only need to describe the elimination of passions, if it was but a negative moment in virtue's progress. "If it is not in essence sinful, then dispassion too, acquires a positive significance—the purification of passion rather than its elimination." [39]

Passion, negatively conceived, is human energy that is directed to an inadequate end. The path whereby passion becomes vice is at least similar to that of virtue's acquisition. For this reason, passion may be reconceived and redirected to overcome vice and acquire virtue. Both moments—negative and positive—are found in *The Ladder*. Passions and virtues exist in the same arena. In the world described by *The Ladder*, passions are disoriented and blind to the human end. One cannot but be struck by *The Ladder*'s preference for the sinner. "The fall for John is an opportunity for life-giving *penthos* and the true resurrection of the human person." [40]

Those who have redirected their loves and are, therefore, "dispassionate" are called "fools," because they have given up the story of this age—which is full of guile about the human *telos*—and have been renewed after the New Adam, Christ. The humble person has come to see that virtue—as the redirection of misplaced passion—is a result of God's loving revelation of himself as the true end of humanity, the story of the *logos* of life. For this reason, John's virtuous person claims no virtue as his own, and recognizes his likeness to sinners—which "likeness" is his own creation.

While virtue is within human reach, it is not acquired without a guide, a mentor. [41] "A ship with a good navigator," John explains, "comes safely to port." [42] With experience in virtue comes perception, so that only one who has struggled on the ladder of virtue has the vision and critical discernment to be a guide on the way. We read in *The Ladder* that those who have been humbled by their passions should take heart. Even if they tumble by their passions into every pit, even if they are trapped by every snare, even if they suffer every disease, still after their return to health they become a light to all, they prove to be doctors, beacons, pilots. They teach us the characteristics of every malady and out of their own experience they can rescue those about to lapse. [43]

Therefore, John requires mentors to be experienced in the practice of virtue—both its positive and negative moments. [44] The assistance of the mentor is "not by words of counsel alone but by the pattern of his entire life." [45] The mentor not only leads the initiate toward love in *The Ladder*, but is an example of love's transformation.

Worldly love and divine *eros* are similar ways of being in John's *Ladder*. "Passion"—understood as redirected, and not just "dispassion"—is offered as an image of the life of virtue. Throughout *The Ladder* may be found images of erotic love. It would seem that celibate love is not unlike the relationship that might hold in marriage, i.e., an intimate knowing. "Eros is not merely an icon, a symbol or figure of speech but above all an energy, a way, a prototype, a specific mode of existence." [46] No human love excludes God completely. Passion is not the problem, but the sign of an insufficient end. Without Christ, passion is bound to be unnatural, inhuman, and insane.

Love as "the reaching out of a person to another" is the nature of God and of humanity. Alterity is the essence of loving persons. Passions which do not nourish alterity, therefore, are person-defeating. As described in *The Ladder*, "gluttony" is the habit of making everything and everybody a "feast" for one's own ends. Love that is not "for the other," and, at last, the "other" who is God, is a miscarriage of the human person.

Love (step 30) is transfiguring. Love, according to John Climacus, makes the lover to show forth the beloved. Love as a virtue includes everything that is God's to be shared.

Love, by its nature, is resemblance to God, insofar as this is humanly possible. In its activity it is inebriation of the soul. Its distinctive character is to be a fountain of faith, an abyss of patience, a sea of humility. [47]

The ladder is for all to ascend. All are to climb toward that love which will unite every virtue—all of human excellence is garnered and crowned in love. John calls everyone to the place where love, dispassion, and adoption are distinguished by name, and name only. Light, fire, and flame join to fashion one activity. So too with love, dispassion, and adoption. [48]

The union of virtue is found here because

he who loves the Lord has first loved his brother, for the latter is proof of the former. Someone who loves his neighbor will never tolerate slanderers and will run from them as though from a fire. And the man who claims to love the Lord but is angry with his neighbor is like someone who dreams he is running. [49]

"We rightly discover that to which we are deeply committed only by having our lives challenged by others." [50] *The Ladder* has challenged countless Orthodox Christians, and it has done so by weaving a narrative that locates their passions and loves in the context of the Christian narrative. Such challenges do not come from without, but, as described by Stanley Hauerwas, by way of the "narrative that has captured our lives." [51] The narrative woven by *The Ladder* is both captivating and repellent. It is captivating because of its grandeur and elevated view of human potential in the light of God's grace. It is, however, repellent because of its very expectations. [52] It allows us no room to blame the other. The prospect of failure challenges us in just the way that Hauerwas notes above, but the last word cannot only be that we have discovered that to which we are *not* committed.

If narrative forms by structuring a world in which to live, it must also teach how to interpret a path that seems so far beyond us and, for that reason, might be abandoned or defused before it is begun. The danger of stories of virtue is that we will promptly devise a hermeneutics of diffusion, if it points to a way that seems unobtainable. Heroic narratives can be transformed—as Nietzsche has shown—into counternarratives of eccentricity and, thereby, be rejected as unpalatable. The real challenge of a virtue narrative is to display the life of virtue, while presenting a way of positively interpreting our failure at being virtuous. [53] What is required is a narrative that is capable of being suspicious of suspicion. *The Ladder* accomplishes this convoluted task. The compassion and intent of a community of virtue can be seen in the presentation of its stories. Not just persons but a community, its intentions, its notions of power, are also shaped in and by the compassionate sharing of its heros in the retelling of its stories. *The Ladder* tells of and requires a community of love, not one of rejection, condemnation, or power.

Many stories might be sampled from *The Ladder* to illustrate this use of narrative. For my purposes, the story of "The Prison" in step 5 is the most helpful. John tells the story of a "place" where he found collected all of those who are in need of repentance. It is important that he presents all of the "failures" of virtue collected in one "place." Here are those who "could not even make a beginning." [54] The characters of the story are those who "dare not ask for complete forgiveness," (123) because they had failed. They ask one another: "Brothers, are we getting anywhere?" (125). They are, in a word, suspicious of the way of virtue.

The narrative continues with one terrible description after another of failure in the pursuit of virtue. "I came close to despair," John claims, "when I had seen and heard all this among them" (127). He insists, however, that while we might have expected such a place to be the abode of human beings become like animals, what he found was no anger, no vanity, "for grief had done away with their capacity for rage" (124). He found a marvelous humanity. The inhabitants of this narrative "encourage one another saying, 'we must run, brothers, we must run' " (125).

After the recounting of "The Prison," John tells a story within the story of "The Prison." He notes that he stayed for thirty days and returned only to discover that he was changed most of all. He proclaims that "those who have fallen and are penitent are more blessed than those who have never fallen and who do not have to mourn over themselves, because through having fallen, they have pulled themselves up by a sure resurrection" (128). John concludes that this is an example of driving out love by love. This is also an example of the use of narrative to prevent the misinterpretation of a narrative by the forces of conceit.

The propensity to devise a counternarrative, and, thereby, defuse *The Ladder* by describing it as the otherworldly flight of a misogynistic monastic, is overcome by presenting the paragon of virtue, i.e., the author of *The Ladder*, as having been directed aright by spending a symbolic thirty days—just like the thirty rungs of *The Ladder*—in a "prison" where love is purified and "failure" becomes the way to virtue. Virtue in this subtle double-narrative cannot be described as a love of self or as an attempt to gain control over the other. It is not an unattainable, overly elevated view of humanity that is encountered in these narratives, but the story of passion finding rest in alterity.

Returning to the point made by Hauerwas that we discover what we are committed to by being challenged by the narrative that has captured our lives, the narrative of "The Prison" challenges our commitments and any stratagem that such virtue is being rejected for any other reason than that we love the sources of our vices. *The Ladder* requires that we ask the eminently practical question of the ways of our loves. The way of virtue so described entails the experience of the failure of misdirected loves, i.e., of "loves" that simply do not give life. These narratives also ensure that the self-description of this community of virtue remains accessible, compassionate, and self-critical by proclaiming "failures" as its "heroes." [55]

Having established the importance of virtue for the Greek Fathers in chapter 2, and further specified the elements of an Orthodox Christian virtue ethic as presented in *The Ladder*, I will next examine the place of virtue in contemporary Orthodox Christian ethics. It has been written that there are now three basic English-language resources for Orthodox Christian ethics: Stanley Harakas, Vigen Guroian, and Christos Yannaras. [56] I will consider each of them in turn.

NOTES

1. *John Climacus: The Ladder of Divine Ascent* (trans. Colm Luibheid and Norman Russell), 290.

2. Ibid., 1.

3. Ibid., 15.

4. Ibid., 10–11.

5. John Breck, *The Power of the Word* (New York: St. Vladimir's Seminary Press, 1986), 55.

6. James D. Chansky, "Reflections on *After Virtue* After Auschwitz," *Philosophy Today* 37 (Fall 1993): 247–256, at 250.

7. John Chryssavgis, "Love and Sexuality in the Image of Divine Love," *The Greek Orthodox Theological Review* 36 (1991): 341–352.

8. *Ladder*, 287.

9. To be blessed with a good genius (*eu-daimon*), hence to be happy. Henry Liddell and Robert Scott, *Greek-English Lexicon* (Oxford: Clarendon, 1964). Also see Aristotle, *Nicomachean Ethics*, 1.4.1.

10. *Ladder*, 257.

11. While there are a total of thirty steps in *The Ladder*, it is helpful to think of the thirty as being constitutive of three major moments: first, a break with the world; second, the elimination of vices that prevent union with God; third, union with God. Richard T. Lawrence, "The Three-Fold Structure of the Ladder of Divine Ascent," *St. Vladimir's Theological Quarterly* 32 (1988): 101–118.

12. *Ladder*, 77.

13. It also functions in a way that is not familiar to moderns, for whom repentance seems to be primarily psychological and therapeutic. In a text influenced by the recent turn to virtue, we read that for Christians "forgiveness must be embodied in a way of life, a life marked by specific practices that enable us to unlearn patterns of sin, to repent for specific sins, and to foster habits of holy living." L. Gregory Jones, *Embodying Forgiveness: A Theological Analysis* (Grand Rapids: William B. Eerdmans Publishing Company, 1995), 49.

14. *Ladder*, 130.

15. The first steps do not, of necessity, lead to meekness; "mourning" and the "remembrance of death" may result in anguish and bitterness over human finiteness. As such, anger is a human response to the threat of death, according to Olivier Clément, *The Roots of Christian Mysticism* (New York: New City Press, 1995), 160–161.

16. *Ladder*, 149.

17. Ibid., 148.

18. Ibid., 151.

19. The primary obstacle to *theosis*—both in the"beginning" and in the present—is, according to Eastern Christianity, "self-love." See, for example, Archimandrite Sophrony, *The Principles of Orthodox Asceticism* in *The Orthodox Ethos* (Oxford: Holywell Press, 1964), 272.

20. *Ladder*, 150.

21. A contemporary definition of chastity would no doubt include the notion that it is a state to be preserved with difficulty, something to be lost, and a negative-condition in the sense that it pertains to what is *not* to be engaged in. In *The Ladder*, by contrast, chastity is not so much a condition to be preserved in its negative moment, as much as it is an eminently practical skill at discerning the *telos* of God. It is gained with others, and not simply sustained by being alone. As such, marriage would seem a practical context for teaching chastity. I will make just such a suggestion in chapter 6.

22. *Ladder*, 173.

23. Julia Annas, *The Morality of Happiness* (Oxford: Oxford University Press, 1993), explains that in classical thought virtue "is built up from repeated choices and the development of habits of choice" (p. 51).

24. *Ladder*, 194.

25. "Fear is not always an evil," according to Constantine Cavarnos, *The Hellenic-Christian Philosophical Tradition* (Belmont, Massachusetts: Institute for Byzantine and Modern Greek Studies, 1989), "a negative emotion, a 'passion.' Thus, 'fear of God' is viewed as something good, as a positive emotion. This is distinguished by the Greek Fathers into two kinds: that of beginners and that of the perfect"(p. 84).

26. *Ladder*, 200.

27. See Justin Popovich, *Orthodox Faith and Life in Christ* (Belmont, Massachusetts: Institute for Byzantine and Modern Greek Studies, 1994), 166. Popovich claims no less than that what "is true for the virtues is true also for knowledge. As each virtue begets other virtues, and begets knowledge, so each sort of knowledge begets another. One virtue produces another and sustains it, and the same is true of knowledge." Popovich holds that knowledge is not possible without virtue.

28. *Ladder*, 217.

29. "Christian ascesis is distinct from 'techniques' of self-control, serenity, inner life, that enable one to enjoy a methodically acquired euphoria; it is at the service of a personal relationship. Personal loyalty to a hidden and revealed personal presence requires faith and humility, which are therefore the most important thing. Humility is not the will to be nothing in order to become all: Rather it is the acceptance of self in openness to the Other." Olivier Clément, *Roots of Mysticism*, 149.

30. *Ladder*, 223.

31. Gk. *Apatheia* (literally, no-passion) means in *The Ladder* not an absence of passion, but the absence of misdirected passion.

32. *Ladder*, 282.

33. "Spiritual progress has no other test in the end, nor any better expression, than our ability to love. It has to be unselfish love founded on respect, a service, a disinterested affection that does not ask to be paid in return, a 'sympathy,' indeed an 'empathy' that takes us out of ourselves enabling us to 'feel with' the other person and indeed to 'feel in' him or her." *Roots of Mysticism*, 270.

34. *Ladder*, 286.

35. *Roots of Mysticism*, 81.

36. In this claim, John Climacus is very much like his predecessor Gregory of Nyssa. Anthony Meredith, *The Cappadocians* (Crestwood, New York: St. Vladimir's Seminary Press, 1995), notes that in *Life of Moses* Gregory is concerned primarily with virtue. "For him, God is not only good and virtuous, he is virtue"(p. 61). Gregory's argument is that "we can only become like God in his infinite virtue by our own continuous striving to be like him"(ibid.). Meredith claims that Gregory arrived at a position that "Christian excellence was ethical rather than mystical"(p. 69).

37. This is because "there is nothing such as an 'independent nature' in the theology of the Greek Fathers. 'Nature' always depends on 'super-nature,' God. God's grace (energies) is necessary in order for 'nature' to continue to be authentic. Nature deprived of grace is no longer true, authentic nature" according to Maximos Aghiorgousis, "Christian Existentialism of the Greek Fathers: Persons, Essence, and Energies in God," *The Greek Orthodox Theological Review* 23 (1978): 15–41, at 31.

38. John Chryssavgis, *Ascent to Heaven: The Theology of the Human Person According to St. John of the Ladder* (Brookline, Massachusetts: Holy Cross Orthodox Press, 1989), 181.

39. Ibid., 181–182.

40. Ibid., 183.

41. "Persons morally mature and hence possessors of experience with respect to the acquisition and exercise of virtue," according to Constantine Cavarnos, *Hellenic-Christian Tradition*, 56.

42. *Ladder*, 259.

43. Ibid., 231.

44. This demand would seem to indicate that other sorts of Christian practices in pursuit of virtue would require a mentor specifically experienced in that practice. In chapter 6, I will suggest that mentors of marriage seem to be indicated by the Orthodox Christian tradition of virtue and by the ritual of marriage.

45. Hausherr, *Spiritual Direction in the Early Christian East*, xi.

46. Chryssavgis, *Ascent to Heaven*, 189.

47. *Ladder*, 286.

48. Ibid., 287.

49. Ibid., 289.

50. Stanley Hauerwas, "Casuistry as Narrative Art," *Interpretations* 37 (1983): 377–388, at 380.

51. Ibid.

52. We read in an earlier English version of *The Ladder* that it "may well strike a modern reader as repellant rather than helpful." St. John Climacus, *The Ladder of Divine Ascent*, trans. Lazarus Moore with an Introduction by M. Heppell (London: Faber and Faber, 1959), 32.

53. This seems to me to be a particular shortcoming of contemporary versions of virtue ethics. They maintain a "prophetic" renunciation of the world, without a satisfying account of complicity with and compassion for the sins of the world.

54. *Ladder*, p. 122.

55. Robert Wuthnow, *Christianity in the Twenty-First Century* (Oxford: Oxford University Press, 1993), is surely correct to claim that judgments about right and wrong carry weight only if one is a member of a moral community that weighs such judgments. I agree with him that it is only in a community that persons and events may become symbolic, and that even if a hero is a "rugged individualist," it is because the community describes rugged individualism and its uses. More subtly, he is correct to point out that "community may precede the telling of tales, but it is also created in the telling itself" (p. 90). It is, therefore, important to consider how any virtue ethic speaks to, for example, the world, thus constituting itself in/as love or hate.

56. Alexander F. C. Webster, review of *Incarnate Love: Essays in Orthodox Ethics*, by Vigen Guroian, in *St. Vladimir's Theological Quarterly* 33 (1989): 304–307, at 304.

4

The Ethics of Harakas, Guroian, and Yannaras

Here I will consider the thought of three ethicists: Stanley Harakas, Vigen Guroian, and Christos Yannaras. My purpose will be to continue to uncover the elements of an Orthodox Christian virtue ethic. The chapter will include very brief descriptions of each ethicist as prologue to an overview of their contributions to my project, particularly in the area of liturgy as practice and the necessity of community.

STANLEY HARAKAS

Stanley Harakas is a graduate of Holy Cross Greek Orthodox Theological School, where he was the long-time Professor of Orthodox Christian Ethics. He is a graduate of the University of Thessalonike and earned a doctorate in the School of Theology at Boston University. Harakas has published books and articles on issues of social ethics (such as church and state, race relations, war, crime, capital punishment, women's concerns, and poverty) and bioethics (such as genetic screening, genetic engineering, artificial insemination, and death and dying).

Harakas maintains what he understands to be a classical Greek Patristic approach to ethics. His position is a synthesis of the major Greek Orthodox Fathers. He divides the task of Orthodox Christian ethics into the specific *theoria* of ethics and its *praxis*. By *theoria* he means the theoretical foundations of ethics, i.e., the knowledge of God and truth. "The *Theoria* of Orthodox Christian Ethics," Harakas writes, "is, without question, inextricably bound up with the doctrinal formulations of the church." [1] But the *theoria* is not simply for ethicians a reproduction of church dogmatics; it is, rather, a matter of discerning those principles of faith that might guide *praxis*, i.e., ethical activity. Harakas notes: "It is the specific *Theoria* which, in turn, provides the guidelines and the direction for the determination of the *Praxis*, i.e., the 'virtuous practice' and the 'correction of habits' and the 'ethical part' of the

Christian life." [2] Harakas requires, however, that the necessary distinction between theory and practice never become more than a conceptual separation. The separation of theory and practice is claimed by Harakas to be essentially methodological.

"Christian ethics," Harakas writes, "is not a sectarian ethic." [3] There is for Orthodox Christianity a certain "continuity between natural ethics (creation) and revealed ethics (redemption)." [4] An Orthodox Christian ethic is rooted in creation, and it includes a good world created by God, the revelation of a new life, and the possibility of a common, i.e., nonrevelatory, ethical life with its philosophical understanding. There is then for Harakas, so to speak, a "canon" for Orthodox ethics that includes major and minor sources. Philosophical ethics would be a part of the canon, albeit for Orthodox Christians it would be a deuterocanonical source. There are, as explained by Harakas, natural precepts basic to any human society.

In an article that serves well as an overview of the position of Harakas, he notes that "few have looked to Eastern Orthodoxy as a source of ethical teaching." [5] He does not find this at all surprising, inasmuch as "one will search in vain the writings of the Church Fathers for systematic treatments of Orthodox Christian ethics." The systematic study of ethics among Greek Orthodox Christians, according to Harakas, began only in the last century. He considers these first attempts to have been patterned primarily on Western prototypes. Harakas favors the form of ethics which

> sees Orthodox Christian ethics as arising out of the fundamental Orthodox Christian view of God, humanity, and the world. It seeks to determine what human beings ought to do in terms of their understanding of what they are, and what they are intended for, as understood within the framework of the apophatic theological faith of the Orthodox Church. [6]

This is the general approach that will circumscribe his ethics.

The essential elements of an Orthodox Christian ethic as presented by Harakas include the following: God in essence is unknowable, but God's relatedness to creation, i.e., God's energies, can be known. This is the apophatic approach so characteristic of Orthodox Christianity. Further, humanity is freely created in the image and likeness of God. "Image" refers to the divine in humanity, and "likeness" to the freedom to complete and fulfill the call to *theosis* or divinization. One may chose not to answer the call of God and, so, weaken the image of God. Christ saves by restoring the image of God in us. Christ is humanity restored, as willed by the Father. The eschatological church is the prototype for society. All of creation is being saved in Christ.

Harakas summarizes how such an ethic functions as follows: "In the condition in which we find ourselves now as a world, as individuals, as society, we stand in a tension between what is and what ought to be." [7] We are ethical, according to Harakas, when striving to achieve the "ought" of God's will. Harakas writes:

> Conceptually then, what we have are certain levels of experience as we seek to live this tension out in our present existence. In the face of chaos, we will insist on the application of the moral law, but if the natural law is functioning well, we would move to the implementation of the Christ-image wherever possible. The Christ-image presupposes the basic order of life and society, but it does not rest on it. It seeks wherever possible to transform it, to transfigure it, to shoot it through with the uncreated Light of God. [8]

The article outlined above contains, in brief, the essential elements for Harakas's much fuller presentation of Orthodox Christian ethics in *Toward Transfigured Life*. In that text can be found a congenial atmosphere for a retrieval of an Orthodox virtue ethic. In the subsection entitled "A Synopsis of Orthodox Christian Ethics," Harakas, having presented essentially the points outlined above, claims that,

> The teachings just sketched out, provide the essential framework for Orthodox Christian ethics. The reciprocal relationships of God and true human life provide for an "ought" based not on the facts of a fallen humanity, but on a "telos" or goal toward which we are called to strive in order to achieve our authentic humanity. [9]

Harakas completes his synopsis by identifying God as the good and *theosis* as the *telos* of humanity. Evil and sin have damaged the image of God in humanity, but have not extinguished the human moral capacity. Human beings are ethically self-determining (*autexousion*), but this moral self must be "cultivated and educated, trained and developed." [10] Discernment (*diakrisis*) is the virtue of what is fitting and appropriate. The "Politea of Theosis" is the community within which are the practices (*askesis*) of the life in Christ. Harakas writes:

> The road to Theosis demands a transfiguration and transformation of life. On the personal level this refers to the development of good character so that it embodies in our "being" a God-like mode of existence.

The cultivation of the virtues and elimination of the vices is seen in the light of "Christian being." The virtues and vices are perceived as modes of that being, the fitting (in the case of the virtues) or the inappropriate (in the case of the vices) modes of being are respectively characterized as virtues and vices. There is a tradition in Eastern Christianity calling for the Imitation of Christ and the saints, not of course, in a slavish external way, but in a deep inner fashion which speaks to the issue of "being" rather than doing. [11]

Harakas's text does not attempt to be more than formal. There is little material application of just how an ethic works its way out in the Orthodox Christian people inhabiting a post-Constantinian, pluralistic society. [12] It must be remembered, however, that the text *Toward Transfigured Life* was to be the "theory" of an Orthodox Christian ethics and not the "practice."

The companion piece to Harakas's *Toward Transfigured Life* is *Living the Faith*. This is another book filled with elements that encourage the development of what might be called a material—rather than, primarily, a formal—Orthodox Christian virtue ethics. Harakas seems, however, unwilling to move very far beyond *theoria*. *Living the Faith* is expressly called the *praxis* of the faith, and Harakas intends this work "to develop a comprehensive practical, livable Orthodox Christian ethic of personal and ecclesial life." [13] He seems to want to combat what he calls a "strong current tendency in Orthodox theology—based on an extreme philosophically conditioned theological existentialism—to minimize this aspect of the life of the Orthodox Church." [14] It is, perhaps, because Harakas sees a danger in so stressing practice—or the existential—that theory is eclipsed, that he finds it difficult to move very far from the formal and theoretical.

Again Harakas emphasizes the transformation of character toward divine likeness (the *telos*) in virtue, but the emphasis is almost as formal in *Living the Faith* as it was in *Toward Transfigured Life*. For example, Harakas understands that "the major 'political' activity of the Church is the *formation of Christian character* in its members"; [15] but this formation seems to have no more content than that characters so formed will "contribute to leading the whole of society toward an appropriate and ethical life." [16] While Harakas insists that *praxis* and *theoria* be interrelated, he seems unwilling to entertain practice-driven, inductive modes of thought that would risk the certainty of moral pronouncements. Theory clearly is the stronger force in his ethics, thus the formalism. Despite this reservation, it is from Harakas that the basic form for any further exploration of an Orthodox Christian virtue ethics can be distilled. The outline of such an Orthodox Christian ethics would include the assertion that there is an "ought" at the very root of the Christian life. This is to claim that there is a *telos* and that the *telos* of the Christian life is found in striving toward *theosis* or deification. The *telos* of deification in Christ demands a transfiguration and transformation of life. This transformation is the development of character so that it embodies a godlike mode of existence. The cultivation of the virtues will be seen in the light of Christian being. Liturgy is the ontological prerequisite or practice of the Christian way of being. The virtues are the modes of fitting Christian being gained in liturgy. There is a tradition of imitation, of exemplars, of saints to be followed. All of which means that an Orthodox Christian ethics speaks to the issue of being, of striving after God and of transformation.

VIGEN GUROIAN

Vigen Guroian is the youngest of the three ethicists under consideration. Guroian began his academic research in the area of Protestant theology. His doctoral dissertation at Drew University was on Reinhold Niebuhr and Edmund Burke. Guroian notes that a change came at his first teaching post. There he had the opportunity to begin to teach courses in Orthodox Christian theology, and he was encouraged "to draw out the prophetic strains in the Orthodox liturgies and rites and to advance those elements in a critique of the culture." [17]

In the introduction to *Incarnate Love* Guroian outlines his theological task. He wants to locate the resources for an Orthodox Christian ethic as it is available in the Orthodox Christian tradition. Having gathered the resources found in Orthodox Christian theology, spirituality, and, especially, liturgy, he wants to relate those resources to other Christian ethicists, all the while mustering these voices in concert for a critique of the culture. Concerning Orthodox Christian worship, Guroian writes: "I have sought to demonstrate not only the power of such worship to cultivate Christian virtue and form Christian community but its ability as well to expose the sinful deviations and idolatries of the society at large" (7). Orthodox Christianity might make an important contribution to social ethics because of its distinctive ecclesiology. The Orthodox Christian way of being church, as distinctive, can be mined, according to Guroian, for contributions unlike those of Reformation and Catholic Christianity. Guroian's ethics, therefore, can be seen as made up of three steps. The first part of his project is the discernment of the *theanthropic* or christological foundation to salvation. The second element is liturgical: Guroian sees worship as ethics. Third, he employs his theological framework—built on steps one and two—to critique the secular social order.

Guroian notes at the beginning of *Incarnate Love* that virtue is greatly valued in the Orthodox Christian tradition. He claims that the virtuous person for Orthodox Christians is not Aristotle's *spoudaios*, but is, rather, the New Adam, Christ, "the theanthropic being in whom divine love is incarnate and creature is reunited with creator" (13). Guroian explains that Adam had been given the vocation to enjoy life in God, but Adam failed. Christ, however, was able to succeed and so become a new and life-giving Adam. In the New Adam, humanity is called to *theosis* or deification.

Guroian notes further that "morality has to do finally, with the restoration of the image of God in humankind" (15). The traditional Orthodox Christian formula for salvation employs the complementary notions of "image" and "likeness" from the Genesis 1 account. Guroian summarizes:

> *Image* connotes that each individual human being is an integral personality having reason, free will, and moral responsibility. Each person is by God's own creative act a subject free to affirm and fulfill humanity. *Likeness* connotes vocation, exercise, virtue, and growth. *Theosis* is not achieved in a moment of conversion. Rather it is accomplished through a lifetime of constant striving and maturing (16).

As presented by Guroian, Christ is the paradigm of the ethically human. He is the God-man in whom life is reunited to the divine. Ethics and salvation are, therefore, intimately connected by Guroian. As an example of this connectedness, Guroian offers the observation that "ethics cannot be done without particular attention to sacramental and liturgical theology" (16). Guroian—as does Harakas—considers liturgy to be the locus for the event of human transfiguration.

The goal of salvation is the Kingdom of God. Guroian maintains that while the Kingdom is beyond ethics—inasmuch as it is beyond all duty, right, or obligation—still, "in a world for which the Kingdom is not fully present, the perfection of persons in their social relations is the appropriate goal of human striving" (23).

The problem of ethics as described by Guroian is just how this Kingdom/society relationship is to be realized. The problem stems from the differing experiences of church that might be offered. Guroian claims that the Orthodox Christian experience of church includes three perceptions about the world. These perceptions are that the world is God's creation, that the sanctified life present in the church displays the world's fallenness, and that it is the call of the church to sanctify all things.

Guroian concludes that there is a distinctive Orthodox Christian ethic that is derived from the life of faith; but that as primarily lived, any such ethic is not likely to be very systematic. Here we find an ethic that risks being practice-driven, unlike that of Harakas; but as such it is also more difficult to judge as compatible or not with Orthodox Christian *theoria*.

However unsystematic such an ethic might be, Guroian is certain that "the theological concepts of *theosis*, image and likeness, and love lie at the heart of the ethic" (27). When Guroian looks to Orthodox trinitarian theology, he finds love to be the fundamental controlling notion. If the Trinity is both archetype and goal for mankind, then trinitarian love and its acquisition is the virtue or excellence central to Orthodox Christian ethics. When Guroian looks to Orthodox Christian liturgy as formative of Christian virtue, he expects to find liturgy shaping persons in communion for love. For Guroian, trinitarian love is the end or *telos* of church and of society.

Guroian observes that among Christian moralists there is seldom concern with *lex orandi*. Ethics as it is usually done today sees little of importance in religious ritual. However, Orthodox Christians, Guroian announces, see the human being as "above all else, a worshiping creature whose very act of worship, if it is not perverse, is to establish and deepen belief and to do good" (52). Guroian applauds Stanley Hauerwas for having moved ethics away from the vain attempt at objective evaluation of acts and toward virtue and character, derived from the context of communal convictions. Liturgy, Guroian explains, serves just that purpose. "It means," he writes, "a gathering whose unifying purpose is to serve (minister to) the world on behalf of God" (53).

As an example of an Orthodox Christian ethic that is liturgically grounded, Guroian looks at the Orthodox Christian sacraments of initiation: baptism, chrismation, and Eucharist. While baptism and chrismation initiate one into the witnessing Body of Christ, it would be incomplete apart from the eucharistic gathering. To die to sinful humanity is, also, to join oneself to the flesh of the Savior. Church membership means community formation, and it is above all, Guroian writes, borrowing a phrase from Hauerwas, a "peculiar community." Church is for Guroian and for Hauerwas a community incommensurable with the world. Guroian requires that church be "a community whose character . . . ought to contrast markedly with that of the world" (65). It seems clear that if liturgy is to teach, i.e., to be practical, then for Guroian its pedagogy is particularly critical towards the world. Guroian maintains that "contrary to the usual emphasis placed by anthropologists and sociologists on the stabilizing or legitimating functions of ritual, Christian liturgy can also function as a criteriological activity which brings judgment—even radical judgment—to bear on a particular social order" (72). The Divine

Liturgy, or eucharistic liturgy, is, Guroian insists, the very shape of a "Christian ethic which challenges the world with the standards of the Kingdom" (75).

Guroian's concern in *Incarnate Love* seems to be with the perceived threat of American culture and with the necessity of a counterattack. "The issue," Guroian contends, "is not primarily sociological, *it is an ecclesial one*" (81). He is not intent on recovering virtue for the good of the culture, but for the good of a church that ought not to be commensurable with American culture. Guroian takes up, at this juncture, a critique of the Orthodox Christian ethicist Stanley Harakas, seen by Guroian as too concerned with the American social order. Guroian explains that Harakas is mistaken if he assumes that Orthodox Christian values can find a place in America. America is not, according to Guroian, ordered to Christian ends. In words that evoke Alasdair MacIntyre, Guroian complains that America is "a highly secularized, pluralistic society, informed by a variety of religious and philosophical traditions" (83). Guroian charges Harakas with the error of Constantinianism. [18] Constantinianism is, according to Guroian, "thinking of social ethics as a special branch of the empire or the nation." [19]

The virtue ethic developed by Guroian in *Incarnate Love* ends with a selection of essays all of which attempt to display the degree of church accommodation to secularism. The primary point of this collection, as voiced by Guroian, is that Orthodox Christians tend to "oppose" the secular order in terms used by the secular order and in so doing capitulate to it. Inasmuch as the peculiar ecclesiology of Orthodox Christianity is seen by Guroian to be the witness of the church to the world, he takes Orthodox Christianity to task for violating its own ecclesial vision of church order. Again, Guroian seems primarily concerned with the impending conversion of Orthodox Christianity by an immensely powerful Western secularism. He writes on the last page of *Incarnate Love*: "Lamentably, the Orthodox parish has taken on a life largely autonomous of and unrelated to the life of worship and prayer." [20] He further notes that "the Orthodox Parish needs to be transformed." [21]

While he seems almost as pessimistic about American culture as Stanley Hauerwas, Guroian's prescriptions are qualified by his Christology and ecclesiology, united to an ancient liturgical tradition. In *Ethics After Christendom*, he does continue to critique an America whose "culture once deeply informed by biblical faith is fast losing its memory." [22] He still considers ethics to belong to the church, although others may see the truth "in limited but crucial ways." [23] Guroian is, however, now more willing to consider "Christians speaking selectively for or against specific public policies in the language of the culture." [24] Nevertheless, as elsewhere, his "principal point here is that in the present situation, the churches are being called not to new projects of culture formation but to habits of virtuous living." [25] Ever richer descriptions of those "habits of virtuous living" uncovered in Orthodox Christian resources by Guroian seem, to me, to be more promising than his social stance. From *Ethics After Christendom* to *Life's Living Toward Dying* Guroian makes substantial progress in describing an ethic of virtue that is characteristically Orthodox Christian. In *Life's Living Toward Dying,* [26] for example, Guroian engages the subject of euthanasia from the perspective of the virtue of "remembering death." To "remember death" is a virtue often invoked in Orthodox Christian texts, but seldom adequately explained. Guroian manages to unpack a little-understood—and even less appreciated—virtue in order to orient Christian practice in regard to euthanasia. Death, he concludes, is not adequately measured by life, but, rather, life is best assayed by death, by dying to what is not of God.

Guroian's work signals an important turn in recent approaches to Orthodox Christian ethics. His books have, essentially, coupled the recent turn to virtue with an Eastern ecclesiology and Christology. These elements distinguish Guroian from all other virtue ethicists.

CHRISTOS YANNARAS

Christos Yannaras, born in 1935, holds doctorates from the Sorbonne and from the Theological School of Thessalonike. He has been influenced by Sartre and Heidegger, and his work attempts to correlate existentialism and Patristic theology. [27] His project can be thought of, conveniently, in three parts. First, Yannaras asks for the characteristic ethos of humanity. Second, he attempts to uncover the existential presuppositions of that ethos. Last, Yannaras asks how transformation toward the characteristically Orthodox Christian ethos is accomplished.

Prior to seeking the characteristic ethos of personhood, Yannaras attempts to clear the ground by unmasking mistaken understandings of ethos. On the very first page of *The Freedom of Morality*—and continuing to the last page—Yannaras rejects any objective yardstick for fulfilled personhood, most especially what he calls virtue. Virtue is understood by Yannaras to be any code of behavior that is beyond dispute. He sees virtue as a bourgeois standard of conduct that is either authoritarian or conventional. Morality when understood in this way leaves humanity with an either/or situation in which the only choice is to select one pole or the other. Yannaras is indicating that human virtue or excellence—conventionally understood—situates a person between a consequentialist or deontological mode of being; both are rejected by Yannaras. Whether one selects a conventional or authoritarian ethics, one "separates the ethos or morality of man, his individual behavior and value as a character, from his existential truth and hypostatic identity—from what man *is*, prior to any social or objective evaluation of him" (14).

Yannaras seems to be taking up a stance like that of the virtue ethicists surveyed, yet he rejects virtue. The key to understanding Yannaras is in the claim that any contemporary conception of morality separates ethos as act from ethos as character. What must be understood, according to Yannaras, is that

> ethics leaves outside its scope the *ontological* question of the truth and reality of human existence, the question of what man really *is* as distinct from what he *ought* to be and whether he corresponds to this "ought" (14).

In humanity's "is" or existence there can be found that which is distinctive of, and, so, determinative of how character ought to be directed towards fulfillment. If there is no human identity prior to character and behavior, according to Yannaras, then morality is merely conformity to authority or to convention.

Contemporary morality is seen by Yannaras as an evasion of the human question, and in this last evasion humanity "wears a mask of behavior borrowed from ideological or party authorities, so as to be safe from his own self and the questions with which it confronts him" (15). Morality is either the realization of what constitutes the fullness of human existence or is a distortion of self by evading humanity's true hypostasis. Morality, according to Yannaras, is to gain one's proper ethos. He maintains that for one "to be *saved* means that he becomes 'safe and *sound*,' or *whole*, and realizes to the full his potential for existence and life beyond space, time and conventional relationships: It means conquering death" (15).

Here is to be found the particularly human characteristic or ethos that grounds the ethics or morality of Christos Yannaras. If salvation is what humanity requires, and if salvation is existence beyond convention, then the ground or starting point is "freedom from any schematic valuation of utilitarian predisposition" (15). Such freedom or salvation can be found, as the source of the characteristic being of humanity, only in the source of all being, only in God.

Yannaras now needs to inquire into the ethos or characteristic way of being of the trinitarian God, as understood by Orthodox Christians, in order to advance his inquiry into the ethos of humanity. Yannaras contends that the ethos of the God worshiped by Orthodox Christians is found in a communion in being that does not stem from essence, but from the personal existence of God the Father, who constitutes his essence in an hypostasis begetting the Son and causing the Spirit to proceed. He writes that "God the Father's *mode of being* constitutes existence and life as a fact of love and personal communion" (18). Therefore, the ethos of God is that God's person precedes his essence or nature. "Being issues not from the essence, which would render it an ontological necessity, but from the person of the Father who in the freedom of his love 'hypostatises' being into a Trinitarian community, begetting the Son, spirating the Holy Spirit." [28]

Humanity is created in the image of God and is one in essence with the rest of humanity, while many in persons. Central to Yannaras's ethics is the insight that humanity in essence is the sum of human nature, but the mode of existence, like that of God, is freedom, personal freedom from all determinations. This freedom is the discerned precondition of morality. Humanity, Yannaras writes, "is capable of either accepting or rejecting the ontological precondition for its existence." [29] Therefore,

> what we call the *morality* of man is the way he relates to this adventure of his freedom. Morality reveals what man *is* in principle, as the image of God, but also what he *becomes* through the adventure of his freedom: a being transformed, or "in the likeness" of God. [30]

If the core of morality as understood by Yannaras is the full acceptance of the being of humanity which is freedom beyond the constraints of nature, then sin is to reject trinitarian communion in favor of human autonomy and self-sufficiency. Yannaras explains the story of the Fall as the bad-faith attempt to deify human nature without God. Morality as it is usually presented, according to Yannaras, is but another temptation to become gods by nature. "From the moment," writes Yannaras, "when the human person rejects this call and this communion in which he himself is grounded, from the moment when he seeks natural and existential autonomy, he becomes alienated from himself." [31] Humanity alienated from its existential self is in need of salvation, of restoration. Salvation demands not a mere change of behavior but existential transformation. This ontological transformation in the direction of trinitarian freedom is, according to Yannaras, "the aim of the Church's ethics." [32] The church is for Yannaras the very path to freedom. In the New Adam, Christ, mankind is restored to his existential self, to freedom, to the image of God.

Any morality or ethics that prompts a person to deny his godlike freedom beyond nature is, according to Yannaras, an existential lie. The proper ethos or character of humanity is to receive the grace of freedom that leads beyond nature to the personal freedom characteristic of trinitarian life as understood by Orthodox Christians. If such freedom is found on the far side of any bourgeois virtue, what would one who is saved look like? Where might one expect to find his "saint"? Where is the exemplar of the ontologically transformed Christian? Yannaras insists that the model is the "fool for Christ." "Fools for Christ" are a particular category of saint in the Orthodox Christian Church. According to Timothy Ware, "fools for Christ" were a sort of saint prominent—though never numerous—in medieval Russia. The "fool" carried the notion of renunciation of worldly wisdom to its furthest extent "by renouncing all intellectual gifts, all forms of earthly wisdom, and by voluntarily taking upon himself the Cross of madness." [33] As described by Yannaras, the way of the fool "is indeed a mockery of the world: it is the most extreme form of asceticism, ultimate self-denial, absolute rejection of the world's standards and complete renunciation of the ego." [34] One should not be misled into thinking that the fools are for Yannaras but exaggerations of fundamental Gospel claims. These saints are the very models of Christian morality. Yannaras summarizes:

> In the case of the fools for Christ, certainly their shocking freedom from every law, rule, restriction or code of obligation is not simply didactic in its purpose, reminding us of the danger of identifying virtue and holiness with conventional social decorum and egocentric moral rectitude. No one can ever really teach simply by calling into question mistaken conceptions and ways of life: one has to make the fullness of the saving truth incarnate in oneself. [35]

We have followed Yannaras from his uncovering of the characteristic ethos of humanity to the existential presuppositions of personal freedom beyond nature as located in the trinitarian life of God. The last step in the project will require that Yannaras describe how one is so transformed, according to the model rendered. The way is found in liturgy. Yannaras holds firmly to a liturgical ethos for humanity. It is in liturgy that one is involved in a new sort of existence that is anchored in trinitarian freedom. Yannaras is able to decode and redescribe every liturgical moment in terms of radical freedom. Whether baptism, marriage, or the eucharistic assembly, liturgy is, according to Yannaras, transformative as access to a mode of being that is beyond nature and found to reside in God's infinite freedom. "We draw near to God," according to Yannaras, "by means of a way of life, not by means of a way of thinking." [36]

SUMMARY

While Harakas, Guroian, and—in particular—Yannaras might well be mined for their differences, I intend to employ them by highlighting certain compatible and complementary claims for any Orthodox Christian ethic. [37]

All three ethicists are alike in that they clearly identify *theosis* or deification as the *telos* of life. Guroian's "love" and the "freedom" identified by Yannaras are both aspects of trinitarian life.

Virtue might be appropriately conceived by Orthodox Christians as the fulfillment of human nature, as in Harakas; as threatening and judging the world, as in Guroian; and even as the final rejection of any human "excellence" that is a captive of nature. Yannaras serves to remind us by his rejection of bourgeois virtue that virtue is ever available as a substitute for salvation. Yannaras cautions against such a transformation, where under the guise of virtue freedom is held captive.

The recreation of all of creation in Christ can be found in all its potential variety in the variously emphasized aspects of Orthodox Christian thought as presented by each ethicist. There is room in the "Politea of Theosis," i.e., the Orthodox Christian community, to include a virtue ethic that is for the life of the world and, so, finds much of value in secular thought and does not reject any human striving as such, while, at the same time, having resources for a critique of the world. So, both Harakas and Guroian can be made to be intelligible in terms of an Orthodox Christian virtue ethic. The community of such an ethic might, I insist, also include Yannaras. It is a community, finally, grounded in the Trinity and destined for the life which is established by the person of the Father, reaching out to and in his Son and Spirit.

In each of the three ethicists considered, the mentors or spiritual guides are selected according to the emphasis desired. The narratives selected from the corpus of Orthodox Christianity also vary only insofar as they are employed to emphasize aspects of church life that the authors wish to address.

Of particular help to our project of clarifying the elements of an Orthodox Christian virtue ethic is the unity found in the common claim of all of these ethicists that the primary practice of transformation is liturgy. All three ethicists consider liturgy to be the practice whereby one enters into a change in the direction of God. The key notion lies in the Orthodox Christian understanding of sacramental "change" that is operating just under the surface in all three of these ethicists.

The "change" that occurs in the eucharistic liturgy—and by extension in all liturgy—is contrasted by Yannaras with change understood as transubstantiation. Orthodox Christians understand the change (*metabole*) as that change which relates *not* to "nature" but to "the mode of existence." [38]

Orthodox Christianity does not contrast "symbol" with "reality," but "symbol" with what is "diabolic." Something is not either real or symbolic for Orthodox Christianity, but either symbolical or diabolical. A "symbol" is that which brings together, makes clear, and unites. *Ballo* means "I cast" or "throw." *Symballo* is to cause to come together, while the opposite is to tear asunder. *Metabole* is the "change" that allows the believer to enter into a way of life where matter is *not* separated from the world as something sacred opposed to that which is not, but is revealed as intended for communion with God.

As Alexander Schmemann has insisted, Orthodox Christians bless water, for example, not to make it "holy water" in contrast to all other water that is profane, but rather to reveal all water as having its true end as communion with God. The world, water, bread, wine, and all of creation, including human-ity, is revealed in sacramental "change" as that which is caught up in the Paschal transformation of recreation in Christ. So, there is an "ought" at the very center of the Orthodox Christian understanding of sacrament: In Eucha-rist *all* bread and wine is revealed as created for communion, but is not yet for me and, so, must be reached for. When gospel narratives of how people of the Kingdom are to exist (i.e., feeding the hungry, etc.) are read, the disjunction between communion with what we are called to be and, yet, are not, energizes the movement toward that *telos*. This sacramental "ought" enlivens Orthodox Christian ethics. The change that is called sacrament or liturgy by Orthodox Christians "is the epiphany—in and through Christ—of the 'new creation,' and not the creation of something 'new.' " [39]

All of which means that the ethicists in question see liturgy or sacrament as the manifestation and experience of church as expectation. All of creation is presented in liturgy as what is in Christ, as communion with the Father in the Spirit, and, yet, as what still must be for me. My "liturgy," or work, is to personally extend this reality to all that I touch in "synergy" with God. My existential "amen" must be added to liturgy. Liturgy as understood by Ortho-dox Christianity is pregnant with the "ought" of God that calls for—even as it is—the new creation. For all three ethicists, as for Schmemann, liturgy is "change" insofar as it is the gift of life transformed. As Yannaras expresses it:

> This does not mean that our nature is taken away within the space of the Kingdom. It means that the way by which our nature is hypostasized (becomes an hypostasis) is transformed. Nature does not become any

longer an hypostasis (a particular living existence) thanks to its own functions and energies, but thanks to the call of God's love. [40]

So as explained by Yannaras, liturgy is the "change" whereby nature—my nature or bread's nature—is revealed as having no life in itself, but only insofar as it has been enhypostasized by Christ. Morality or ethics is, then, for all the progressive personalization of nature as the grace of communion in Christ by the Holy Spirit with the Father; and this ethos is liturgical.

The priority of "community" in such an ethics is starkly sketched out by Harakas who holds that "individualism has never been a dominant theme in Eastern Orthodoxy." [41] Our God is not alone, and virtue or human excellence is also to be found in community. Harakas maintains that Orthodox Christian ethics is communitarian. Community is an essential element for any under-standing of Orthodox Christian ethics. "Human experience of the good," Harakas maintains, "especially in the realization of the image of God is constituted by a divine-human sharing and koinonia." [42] "Orthodox Christian Ethics at heart is relational in character." [43]

The communitarian element in Orthodox Christian ethics is fundamen-tal both because the direction of the striving after virtue, of becoming like God, is in the direction of the trinitarian community of love and because such striving takes place within the community of persons (the church) whose work or liturgy is to become ever more conformed to their God. "Human life," as described by Harakas, "is iconic (reflective) of the divine goodness." [44] The God worshiped by Orthodox Christians—who is the ought of human becoming—is "never only privately or individualistically encountered and realized; realization of *theosis* always has its corporate dimensions." [45]

Guroian echoes the claim that an essential aspect of any Orthodox Christian ethics is community. He notes that when he began to teach ethics in an American college, he discovered that his students offered abundant "evidence of a deeply ingrained individualism and convictions about the primacy of the self." [46] Guroian concluded that the practical morality of most American students offered the autonomous self as "the ultimate irreducible reality." [47]

In contrast to the self as the ground of ethics, Guroian discovered that for Orthodox Christians, the community was the most fundamental ground for doing ethics. "Humanity created in the image of God is a multiplicity of hypostases of a common nature in loving relation with one another." [48] Our contemporary inability to do ethics rests, as seen by Guroian, with a fall from community and its resources.

Yannaras is even more insistent than are either Harakas or Guroian in maintaining the fundamental importance of community for ethics. Yannaras returns conceptually to the Cappadocian Fathers to renew the Orthodox Christian understanding of the fundamental community of the Trinity. Here the unity or community of the Godhead is not to be located in nature but in a person—the person of the Father.

God is one and God is love because the person of the Father reaches out to the Son and Spirit in love and, thus, constitutes the nature of the divine community. Christ saves by enhypostatizing human nature for redemption. In liturgy, we become godlike by receiving (hypostatically) the New Adam. For Yannaras, "person" is the "life-giving principle." [49] God is love (1 Jn 4.16), because "God is a Trinity of Persons." [50] God is community or triadic because, as explained by Yannaras, "each Person exists not for himself, but he exists offering himself in a community of love with other Persons." [51] Christ is a divine Person who constitutes his human nature for the end of love, the love of the Father and of creation. Yannaras rejects ethics that call for a mere psychological change related to some earthly standard. The true ethos, character, or ethics of the human person created in the image of God is to constitute his very nature (which is the "work" of liturgy) in community (which is the church as the gift of trinitarian life).

Community is, then, fundamental to the ground, way, and, as trinitarian, end of any Orthodox Christian ethics according to Harakas, Guroian, and Yannaras. We may conclude further that this communitarian dimension extends, at least for Harakas, even to ground a natural law ethic. There is, he contends, "a pan-human moral standard of behavior." [52] This natural law is what is required to maintain community, i.e., "to sustain the basic institutions of inter-personal and societal living." [53] One might expect to find room for a limited natural-virtue ethic in such a view, and, indeed, just such a stance can and has been located in the early Greek Fathers in our chapter 2. Any such "natural" communitarian ethic, however, would need to be extended to the community of the church, if it were to address the "development of God-like character." [54] A natural-law virtue ethic would "end" where the ought or call to community became unintelligible as merely human, and required the explication of a call to community that was divine. All of humanity, in summary, is necessarily marked by the divine community. The life of the Trinity is our beginning and our end.

John Chryssavgis has noted that for Orthodox Christians "the question of virtues is directly related to that of nature and grace." [55] For any Orthodox Christian ethic concerned with virtue, we would need to concern ourselves with nature and grace, i.e., with "where we have come from" and "where we are going." The next chapter will, for that reason, present a description of the Orthodox Christian understanding of creation and of salvation in Christ. It is our contention that such a description will necessarily imply a virtue ethic. An ethos of virtue is at the core of the Orthodox Christian faith.

NOTES

1. Stanley Harakas, *Toward Transfigured Life: The* Theoria *of Eastern Orthodox Ethics* (Minneapolis: Light and Life Publishing Company, 1983), 2.

2. Ibid.

3. Ibid., 7.

4. Ibid., 9.

5. Stanley Harakas, "Ethics in the Greek Orthodox Tradition," *The Greek Orthodox Theological Review* 22 (Spring 1977): 58–62, at 58.

6. Ibid., 59.

7. Ibid., 61.

8. Ibid.

9. Harakas, *Toward Transfigured Life*, 33.

10. Ibid., 35.

11. Ibid., 36–37.

12. In *Toward Transfigured Life*, Harakas applauds Hauerwas's *Character and the Christian Life.* Harakas sees it as in agreement with the Orthodox Christian anthropology of "image and likeness." Harakas, however, soon finds little to agree with once Hauerwas begins to publish texts that call on American churches to disengage from the "Constantinian" attempt to support a secular order. Church and world are fundamentally incommensurable in Hauerwas's ethics. For Harakas, in contrast to Hauerwas, Constantine was a saint and his name evokes the noble effort of Byzantine Christian civilization to enter into a synergistic relationship with the world, for the life of the world.

13. Stanley Harakas, *Living the Faith: The* Praxis *of Eastern Orthodox Ethics* (Minneapolis: Light and Life Publishing Company, 1992), ix.

14. Ibid., 303–304.

15. Ibid., 361.

16. Ibid., 362.

17. Vigen Guroian, *Incarnate Love: Essays in Orthodox Ethics* (Notre Dame: University of Notre Dame Press, 1987), x.

18. Constantinianism is a term favored by Hauerwas. For the uses of Constantinian, see Stanley Hauerwas, *Vision and Virtue: Essays in Christian Ethical Reflection* (Notre Dame: University of Notre Dame Press, 1981), p. 204ff; also chapter 7, John Yoder, *The Priestly Kingdom: Social Ethics as Gospel* (Notre Dame: University of Notre Dame Press, 1987). In an article reviewing John Yoder's importance for contemporary ethics written by Stanley Hauerwas, "When the Politics of Jesus makes a Difference," *The Christian Century* 110 (1993): 982–987, we read that Yoder's text is a "classic" not because it can be read as a general commentary about essential human truths, but because it teaches Christians to read other texts in the Christian tradition. Guroian

also wants to read America from the text of Orthodox Christianity. This strategy seems to me to be less typical of Orthodox Christianity than that of iconographic representation. That is, God's good creation as rendered "dead" by human choice is personally remembered (recapitulated) to become an icon. For Orthodox Christians the "world" as created is not simply to be rejected, but is of the Kingdom both as realized in Christ and—with undiminished passion—loved as yet to come. Orthodox learn to "remember" everything in light of Christ's nuptial yearning, that of the *nymphios.*

19. Guroian, *Incarnate Love,* 84.

20. Ibid., 178.

21. Ibid.

22. Vigen Guroian, *Ethics After Christendom: Toward an Ecclesial Christian Ethic,* (Grand Rapids: William B. Eerdmans Publishing Company, 1994), 198.

23. Ibid.

24. Ibid., 100–101.

25. Ibid., 101.

26. Vigen Guroian, *Life's Living Toward Dying* (Grand Rapids: William B. Eerdmans Publishing Company, 1996).

27. Christos Yannaras, *The Freedom of Morality,* trans. Elizabeth Briere (New York: St. Vladimir's Seminary Press, 1984), 10.

28. Aidan Nichols, *Light From the East: Authors and Themes in Orthodox Theology* (London: Sheed and Ward, 1995), 183.

29. Yannaras, *Freedom of Morality,* 20.

30. Ibid., 24.

31. Ibid., 30.

32. Ibid., 37.

33. Timothy Ware, *The Orthodox Church* (Baltimore: Penguin Books, 1969), 118.

34. Yannaras, *Freedom of Morality,* 66.

35. Ibid., 74–75.

36. Christos Yannaras, *Elements of Faith: An Introduction to Orthodox Theology,* trans. Keith Schram (Edinburgh: T & T Clark, 1991), 14.

37. By reading Yannaras in this way, I do not mean to dispense with his substantive objections to virtue. The dialectic established by contrasting person with individual and hypostatic existence with nature, which drives his theological ethics, would preclude employing him to support any ethic wherein virtue proceeds from an autonomous nature. Nature ought not determine the person; rather, as in Christ we are free to personalize nature. Yannaras is attempting to maintain and imaginatively extend the Patristic move from Greek ontology to Christian personalism; but if virtue is conceived as the personal appropriation of the grace of the new creation in Christ by the Holy Spirit, then the objections to "virtue" made by Yannaras might well be satisfied. In any case, I find his (Sartre-like) insistence that we are not captive of nature but radically free for the adventure of existence to be throughly Orthodox and not fundamentally at odds with my project, although his blanket rejection of virtue might make it seem so.

38. Yannaras, *Elements of Faith,* 131.

39. Alexander Schmemann, *For the Life of the World: Sacraments and Orthodoxy* (New York: St. Vladimir's Seminary Press, 1988), 143–144.

40. Yannaras, *Elements of Faith*, 73.
41. *Toward Transfigured Life*, 241.
42. Ibid., 240.
43. Ibid.
44. Harakas, *Living the Faith*, 11.
45. Ibid.
46. Guroian, *Ethics After Christendom*, 15.
47. Ibid., 19.
48. *Incarnate Love*, 33.
49. *Elements of Faith*, 32.
50. Ibid., 36.
51. Ibid.
52. *Living the Faith*, 14.
53. Ibid., 15.
54. Ibid.
55. *Ascent to Heaven* (Brookline: Holy Cross Orthodox Press, 1989), 165.

5

From Creation to Salvation

All of the material that has been assembled thus far has indicated that virtue is central to any comprehensive understanding of Orthodox Christianity. Not unlike the view of the Jewish theologian, Abraham J. Heschel, presented in chapter 1, Orthodox Christianity finds at the core of the human experience a dynamic call to what humanity ought to be. There is a call to virtue in human existence, and this summons requires striving in the direction of human completion. The call to strive after virtue is, then, implicit in creation as understood by Orthodox Christianity, and is not, it will be shown, obviated by sin. The journey of virtue moves from out of our creation toward what we are intended to become as created beings. This chapter will present the elements of that dynamic: creation, anthropology, sin, and salvation in Christ, as Orthodox Christianity understands them. From beginning to end, a virtue ethic will be seen to be implicit in Orthodox Christian thought. Indeed, it is our contention that it is impossible to properly appreciate the Church of the Christian East without reference to *arete.*

CREATION

Vladimir Lossky [1] maintains that the Christian understanding of the world's creation from out of nothingness by God's free will is unique among the world's religions. [2] Orthodox Christianity holds neither to the notion of the eternality of matter found in Greek thought, nor to the understanding of creation as a necessary divine procession. Creation is, rather, a free act of God. "It does not," according to Lossky, "respond to any necessity of divine being whatever" (52). God as Trinity is, already, a fullness of love, and has no need for the world as a necessary expression of love. While God is Trinity eternally, God "is not eternally creator, as Origen believed, who, prisoner of the cyclic conceptions of antiquity, therefore made Him dependent on the creature" (53). Nevertheless, "the very being of God is reflected in the creature and calls it to share in His divinity" (53). Lossky summarizes:

> To create is not to reflect oneself in a mirror, even that of prime matter, it is not vainly to divide oneself in order to take everything unto oneself. It is a calling forth of *newness*. One might almost say: a risk of newness. When God raises, outside of Himself, a new subject, a free subject, that is the peak of His creative act. Divine freedom is accomplished through creating this supreme risk: another freedom (54).

According to Georges Florovsky, [3]

> The world exists. But it *began* to exist. And that means: *the world could have not existed*. There is no necessity whatsoever for the existence of the world. Creaturely existence is not self-sufficient and it is not independent. In the created world itself there is no foundation, no basis for genesis and being. Creation by its very existence witnesses to and proclaims its creaturehood. [4]

So, according to Lossky and Florovsky, not only is the creator free, but humanity is likewise free. At the same time, however, and without contradiction, humanity is radically dependent on God. Humanity is free to seek out its proper being, but that being, that meaning, cannot be found in the creation without God.

"The reality and substantiality of created nature is manifested first of all," Florovsky continues, "in *creaturely freedom*" (48). Such a creation is not a mere extension of God's nature, and it is free to be other than God willed it to be. "Creaturely freedom is disclosed first of all," Florovsky continues, "in the equal possibility of two ways: to God and away from God" (48). He concludes that "creation must ascend to and unite with God by its own efforts and achievements" (49). Virtue—or vice—is inherent, therefore, in the very creation of humanity as understood by these Orthodox theologians. "There is no irresistible grace," Florovsky explains, "creatures can and may lose themselves, are capable, as it were, of 'metaphysical suicide' " (49).

Creation is understood by Orthodox Christians to be grounded in trinitarian life. "The Father creates through the Word in the Holy Spirit, says the patristic adage, and St. Irenaeus calls the Son and the Spirit 'the two hands of God.' " [5] Lossky observes that St. Basil the Great maintained that the Father is the primordial cause, the Son is the operative cause, and the Spirit is the perfecting cause. Human being and becoming is grounded in a trinitarian community of Divine Love.

The Son is the Logos because he is the revelation and manifestation of the Father. Each created entity participates in the Divine Logos by having its own "logos" or "essential reason." Therefore, as explained by Lossky, the Divine Logos "gives to the created word not only the order signified by Its name, but its very ontological reality." [6] All of God's creation has its end or purpose in God as Triune. The meaning of creatures is to be found in the Logos. Humanity is, then, created to be a manifestation of the Logos.

Lossky distances the Christian notion of likeness from that of Plato. Platonic "ideas" are the sources of creation and maintain a higher level of being than even the gods, but for the Greek Fathers, "God is not only an intelligence containing divine ideas: His essence infinitely transcends ideas." [7] God does not create a replica of his thought, of himself; and the created world is not an inferior realm. Lossky sees the Greek Fathers as impregnating Platonic terms with "a thoroughly biblical respect for the sensible and the living God." [8] The "ideas" do not determine God's creative act and do not display a higher realm of escape from the sensible. The ideas or *logoi* of Greek Patristic thought elevate the nature of matter and identify the creature as called to participate in its meaning, in its "ought" which is to be found only in God's love. John Meyendorff, agreeing with Lossky, explains: "It has been created in order to 'participate' in God, who is not only the prime mover and the goal of creation, but also the ultimate meaning (*logos*) of its permanence." [9] God is, then, the beginning, the end, and the meaning, the very ethos of humanity, but humanity is also related to the rest of creation.

The six days of Genesis are understood by Lossky as descriptive of "concentric spheres of being at the center of which man, who virtually recapitulates them, finds himself." [10] The orders created by God are the seeds of differentiated, created being. Humanity, however, is not a "part" but a "person." "Free totality, he is born of the 'reflection' of God as free totality." [11] Humanity is not, as understood by Orthodox Christianity, a fragment of the created world, seeking salvation by reunion with it.

Humanity is created male and female. The revelation and mystery of the one and many in humanity is seen by Lossky to reflect the revelation and mystery of the one and many in God. "In the same way that the personal principle in God demands that the one nature express itself in the diversity of persons," he writes, "likewise in man, created in the image of God." [12] Humanity can never be a monad, but is created from and for the communion of community. Only in community could the call to be a person, in the Orthodox Christian sense of the word, be realized.

Florovsky summarizes the Orthodox Christian understanding of creation by explaining that

> there is in creation a supra-natural challenging goal set above its own nature—the challenging goal, founded on freedom, of a free participation in and union with God. This challenge transcends created nature, but only by responding to it is this nature itself revealed in its completeness. This challenging goal is an aim, an aim that can be realized only through the *self-determination* and efforts of the creature. Therefore the process of created becoming is real in its freedom, and free in its reality, and it is by this becoming that what-was-not reaches fulfillment and is achieved. Because it is guided by the *challenging-goal.* [13]

Florovsky's point, it would seem, is that our context is that of a creation made in freedom and love wherein creatures are capable of striving toward the goal or end of union with God. Humanity is truly free to become what it will. It may reach out toward God or not. It is, however, only in the striving that we come to realize what the human is capable of becoming. Human nature is created to be capable of reaching out beyond itself even to divine life.

THE ANTHROPOLOGY OF IMAGE AND LIKENESS

The foundation of Orthodox Christian anthropology is that humanity is created to participate in divine life. To be human is to know God and to grow in that knowledge. "For the entire patristic and Byzantine tradition, knowledge of God implies 'participation' in God—i.e., not only intellectual knowledge, but," according to Meyendorff, "a state of the entire human being, transformed by grace, and freely cooperating with it by the efforts of both will and mind." [14] In the same place, Meyendorff applauds the presentation of Gregory Palamas, a fourteenth-century defender of hesychast monks, that describes the knowledge of God as not simply intellectual or propositional but moral and transformational: "It is impossible to possess God in oneself, or to experience God in purity, or be united with the unmixed light, unless one purify oneself through virtue, unless one get out, or rather above, oneself." [15]

The possibility of climbing above oneself toward God is traditionally expressed in the Orthodox Christian Church in the language of image and likeness. In Genesis 1.27 we read that God created humanity in his own image and after his likeness. Georgios I. Mantzarides notes that "in the works of the fathers and of ecclesiastical authors the term 'image' is used extensively, and many different interpretations of it are forthcoming." [16] Mantzarides lists

Byzantine Church authors who identify the image of God in humanity with intellect, as does Clement of Alexandria, but there are also those who point not only to the intellect but to free will and a long list of bodily gifts, as does Gregory of Nyssa. At the end of his survey, however, Mantzarides maintains that "image" is best understood in the Orthodox Christian tradition as the many-sided, dynamic notion of image found, for example, in the thought of Gregory Palamas. Palamas, like Irenaeus before him, identified "image" with the completely human. [17] For the Orthodox Christian tradition, Adam is created in the image of God and has the power of development toward perfection. Perfection is to become like God, that is, *theosis* or deification. "This movement of man from 'image' to archetype," according to Mantzarides, "is generally expressed in the Fathers by the phrase from the Scripture 'after His likeness.' " [18] In the Greek Septuagint "image" (*icon*) indicates for Orthodox Christians what humanity has to begin with, while "likeness" is that which is to be attained. "Likeness to God, while it constitutes the goal of human experience," Mantzarides explains, "is not imposed on man, but is left to his own free will." [19] The image must be received as a gift to be cultivated. The image is a loving call to virtue in freedom.

Vladimir Lossky maintains that the character of the divine nature in humanity is best explained by insisting that humanity "is a personal being like God." [20] Humanity is not blind or autonomous nature but is properly grasped as made for participation in divinity by virtue of personhood. "To be in the image of God, the Fathers affirm, in the last analysis is to be a personal being, that is to say, a free responsible being" (71). Lossky asks why God made humanity responsible and free: "Precisely because He wanted to call him to a supreme vocation: Deification; that is to say, to become by grace, in a movement boundless as God, that which God is by His nature" (71–72).

While humanity was created in the image of God by the free will of God, all of the aforementioned authors agree, humanity cannot be deified by the divine fiat alone. Lossky simplifies the Orthodox Christian understanding of humanity as: "A single will for creation, but two for deification. A single will to raise up the image, but two to make the image into a likeness" (73). This dimension of Orthodox Christian anthropology is summarized by Lossky by insisting that

> a person, affirming himself as an individual and confining himself to the limits of his separate nature, cannot flower fully and grows impoverished. Only by renouncing his own content, freely giving it up, ceasing to exist for himself alone, does a person fully express himself in the simple

nature of all. Renouncing his separate good, he endlessly expands, and is enriched by everything that belongs to all. A person becomes the perfect image of God by discovering His likeness, which is the perfection of the nature common to all men. The distinction between persons and nature reproduces in humanity the order of divine life, expressed by the dogma of the Trinity. This is the basis of all Christian anthropology, of all evangelical morality, for, according to Gregory of Nyssa, "Christianity is the imitation of God's nature" (128; De Professione Christiana, P.G. 46, col. 244C.).

Lossky clarifies this further by explaining that in the Orthodox Christian view, Adam in his original state was indeed perfect, "yet this does not mean that his original state coincided with the ultimate aim, that he was in union with God from the moment of creation" (130). No, according to Lossky, even the perfection of paradise was an expression of the capacity of Adam to move toward God and commune with divinity. Even in the Garden of Genesis, humanity is to be understood as having a free and dynamic character. In reading Lossky it is impossible not to interpret the task of humanity as involving virtue. The task of being human is found in striving after the virtue found only in God.

Meyendorff adds an important clarification to this anthropology. Concerning the claim that humanity is created to participate in divine life, he notes that inasmuch as humanity is not autonomous, but requires the gift of God by nature, we can claim that "grace" gives humanity its "natural" development. [21] Orthodox Christian theologians take for granted that "true humanity is realized only when he lives 'in God' and possesses divine qualities" (139). In the Orthodox Christian tradition, there is no opposition between nature and grace, between freedom and God.

Although humanity is meant from the beginning for divine life, this does not mean that it is limited in its freedom to realize God by its own efforts. "Divine life is a gift," Meyendorff maintains in agreement with the entire Byzantine tradition, "but also a task which is to be accomplished by a free human effort" (139). A task or "ought" is, therefore, located at the center of Orthodox Christian anthropology. Even before surveying Byzantine Christology, it is evident that virtue or human excellence is at the center of Orthodox Christian thought. We will soon see that for Orthodox Christianity the coming of Christ does not change the goal of creation. Christ comes to make possible the goal of divinization that is obstructed by death, by separation from the God who is our life. Christ is both human virtue and the new possibility for the acquisition of virtue for the many.

SIN AND FALL

John Meyendorff claims that to understand Orthodox Christianity, it is important to realize that Augustine's struggle with Pelagius and Julian of Eclanum had little, if any, influence on the Christian East. He writes: "In the Byzantine world, where Augustinian thought exercised practically no influence, the significance of the sin of Adam and of its consequences for mankind was understood along quite different lines" (143). That difference is significant for locating virtue ethics in Orthodox Christian thought.

Meyendorff notes that communion with God was understood in the East as reaching out for what is above nature. "Nature can and must be transcended"; he explains, "this is the privilege and function of the *free mind*, made 'according to God's image' " (143). "Guilt," for the Greek Patristic tradition, may be incurred only by that which is free and personal. The human person is dynamic and always reaching out either toward God or toward what is not God. "When the human person, or hypostasis, by rebelling against both God and nature misuses its freedom," Meyendorff explains, "it can distort the 'natural will' and thus corrupt nature itself " (143). In freedom, humanity may either strive toward the perfecting of nature in Christ or toward its further destruction, the "death" of nature.

All of the above indicates that for the Eastern Church it is not possible to consider the biblical Fall as other than the "personal" sin of Adam and Eve. In Orthodox Christian anthropology there is no room, according to Meyendorff, for a sin of nature or for inherited guilt. Sin and guilt are always personal, *hypostatic*. Nature, as created, moves toward God; it is *hypostasis* that has the "freedom" to rebel against the proper end of nature. There are, indeed, consequences to the Fall, but the consequences are understood as cosmic and communal. Sin requires the free and personal participation of a given individual. Adam's sin, therefore, is not *my* sin.

Meyendorff furthers his argument concerning the nature of sin in Orthodox Christianity by attempting a Patristic analysis of Romans 5.12, a pivotal text in Christian understandings of sin and its consequences. He maintains that the Latin text of Romans 5.12 translates the Greek words *eph ho pantes hemarton* into *in quo omnes peccaverunt*. The result of this translation is that the Latin text can be read to support a notion of inherited guilt. The text might be read as claiming not only that Adam sinned and brought death into the world to spread to all, but that he is the one *in quo*, in whom, *omnes peccaverunt*, all have sinned. This would be, according to Meyendorff, a "sin of nature." The Greek text cannot be rendered in this fashion.

Eph ho, Meyendorff explains, is a contraction of *epi ho*, and is more correctly translated as "because." Meyendorff suggests that such a rendering, compatible with most Byzantine Church authorities, would result in Paul's words being understood as claiming that Adam's sin brought death, as its wage, into the world; and because of death, all of us sin. Such an understanding, according to Meyendorff, "presupposes a cosmic significance of the sin of Adam, but does not say that his descendants are 'guilty' as he was, unless they also sin as he sinned" (144).

Therefore death is a cosmic disorder in human existence that has been brought to pass by the choice of one person, but it holds all of the community of humankind under its power. Life has been murdered from the beginning (Jn 8.44), and death, which now rules, makes for personal sin and the further corruption of nature. We have, according to Orthodox Christianity, inherited a "condition." [22] "There is indeed," Meyendorff contends, "a consensus in Greek patristic and Byzantine traditions in identifying the inheritance of the Fall as an inheritance essentially of mortality rather than of sinfulness, sinfulness being merely a consequence of mortality." [23] Thus the distinction between the first Adam and Christ, the second Adam, according to Meyendorff, "is seen in terms not of guilt and forgiveness but of death and life." [24]

Vladimir Lossky explains that for the Fathers evil is understood as a vice or imperfection. "Evil is not a nature," he insists, "but a state of nature, as the Fathers would say most profoundly." [25] As considered by Lossky, sin is a free—thus, *hypostatic*—revolt against God's call to human completion. The contamination of sin is not, therefore, automatic. "It could not be propagated," Lossky insists, "except through the free acquiescence of human will" (81).

Lossky places the source of sin in human pride. The root of the Fall is grounded in the mistaken desire for self-deification. Sin is, according to Lossky, "the hatred of grace" (82). It is the rejection of divine community, and its inherent call for free beings to strive after their end which is the sharing of trinitarian life in love. Not to strive in this fashion is to attempt to maintain nature without grace. Since humanity is created, from the beginning, for the gift of trinitarian life, we become "non-natural," according to Lossky, when we thus sin (82).

Into this disorder, God introduces a certain order. Pedagogy, Lossky holds, is God's response to the disintegration of humanity. "Adam was directly called to deify himself" (83). The Fall, according to Lossky, resulted in two obstacles to inhibit such striving after perfection. He maintains, agreeing with Meyendorff, that death and sin render humanity incapable of attaining their true end. Death distorts reality. This condition results in our missing the mark and in "growing" not toward God but away from our true end.

While the condition of humanity has changed, "God's plan has not changed" (84). If the first Adam has failed, the second Adam will succeed. Salvation in Christ is not, Lossky makes abundantly clear, the goal, as understood by Orthodox Christianity. Rather, the goal is union with God. After falling from communion with God, humanity cannot reach the proper end of its striving, but in Christ the striving after human perfection can be begun again. In Christ the creation is renewed. With the coming of Christ, according to Lossky, "begins a new period when human persons, supported by the Holy Spirit, must freely acquire . . . deification" (85).

CHRIST AND SALVATION

The goal that humanity be united to divinity has not changed with the Fall, according to Lossky, and must not be severed from the economy of the Son (119). The deification of humanity is still the end of Divine Love, but the Fall requires a change in what Lossky calls the divine pedagogy (110–111). What has changed, he explains, is that

> sin has destroyed the primitive plan, that of a direct climb of man to God. A catastrophic fracture has opened in the cosmos; this wound must be healed and the abortive history of man redeemed for a new beginning: such are the aims of redemption (111).

Salvation in Christ is, therefore, salvation for striving after the end of human excellence which is deification. "It is first," according to Lossky, "the abolition of radical obstacles which separate man from God" (111). It is the destruction of all that might prevent the free striving of humanity toward *theosis.* "This liberation," he continues, "of the captive creature is later accompanied by a restoration of his nature, rendered capable of receiving grace and going from 'glory to glory,' even as far as that likeness which takes unto it the nature divine, and allows it to transform the cosmos" (111).

John Meyendorff echoes the view of Lossky that humanity was called to the virtue of deification and, thereby, to call all of creation to God. The cosmic catastrophe of the Fall could be corrected only by the creator. The redemption of creation—its recreation—occurred in Christ. [26] Meyendorff contends that

> the fact of the Incarnation implies that the bond between God and man, which has been expressed in the Biblical concept of "image and likeness," is unbreakable. The restoration of creation is a "new creation," but it does not establish a new pattern, so far as man is concerned; it reinstates *man* in his original divine glory among creatures and in his original responsibility (152).

In Christ the creation that was torn from life and turned toward death is renewed. Meyendorff explains that

> in the person of Christ, in the sacramental reality of His Body, and in the life of the saints, the transfiguration of the entire cosmos is antici-pated; but its advent in strength is still to come. This glorification, however, is indeed already a living experience available to all Christians, especially in the liturgy. This experience alone can give a goal and meaning to human history (153).

Meyendorff is very careful to add that in Christ humanity is not over-come or absorbed. In Christ what is found is the conformity of the human will to the divine will. In Christ the death that has overshadowed all human striving is overcome by life and, thus, in Christ the human person can again will God's way. This is the restoration of creation and the reopening of the human vocation for excellence. Meyendorff maintains that the "key" to understanding the Eastern Christian view of salvation is to see that "participa-tion" in God's life, deification, is not the overcoming of humanity but is, indeed, the very nature of the human task (153).

Salvation in Christ as explained by Orthodox Christianity is further clarified by noting that Orthodox Christianity holds to an "asymmetrical Christology." The person or hypostasis of Christ is the Logos. The human nature of Christ was not a human hypostasis, but he was a human individual. "A fully human individual life was enhypostasized in the hypostasis of the Logos," according to Meyendorff, "without losing any of its human character-istics" (154). Meyendorff insists that in the Orthodox Christian understanding, the asymmetry of Christ does not detract from the humanity of Christ but reveals the character of the truly human. Following Meyendorff, it is clear that for Orthodox Christianity human virtue is both to be theocentric and to actively move toward God. We are most human, therefore, when we are actively moving toward the life that is found in God.

According to Meyendorff, "Jesus' hypostasis has a fundamental affinity with all human personalities: that of being their *model*" (159). All of humanity is created according to the image of the Logos; and when God assumed the human in Christ, all of humanity had reopened for them the possibility of answering the call to strive after that likeness. The body of Christ is human nature that is not under the dominion of death. In Christ the goal of humanity is accomplished. In Christ my humanity can find trinitarian life and sanctifica-tion. Meyendorff explains that "Byzantine theology did not produce any elaboration of the Pauline doctrine of justification expressed in Romans and Galatians" (160). If there is a sense of "substitution" in Orthodox Christian soteriology, then it is "in the wider context of victory over death and of sanctification" (160). Death is overcome in the assumption of human mortality by the Logos. This is so because "death" is, essentially, separation from God's will.

While he does not develop the claim, Meyendorff insists that Christ's resurrection is the foundation of Christian ethics (162). The human situation after the Fall, its existential condition, is best expressed as one of death and dying. We find ourselves within the context or narrative of death—a story of those who have turned from the source of their life—and, so, we tend practically to respond in life in accord with death's dominion. The Resurrection is proclaimed as freedom from death. We who have been enslaved to death and, so, have not been free, are set free to be human by Christ who has made for us a *Pascha* or "Passover" from death to life. Meyendorff writes that in the Resurrection, "death has ceased to be the only possible end of existence, man is free from fear, and sin, based on the instinct of self-preservation, is no longer unavoidable" (162).

This means, concretely, that in the church we can learn to live according to the Resurrection, according to life and not death, and, so, we may strive freely toward our proper end. The gift of redemption is, of course, free, unearned, and available to all, even to children; but the life that is made possible by the life, death, and resurrection of Christ belongs to free choice. The grace or gift of redemption is life; a life that must be lived.

Christ's humanity, Meyendorff explains, is penetrated with the divine. Although Christ's humanity is deified, it does not lose human characteristics. "These characteristics," he holds, "become even more real and authentic by contact with the divine model according to which they were created" (164). This is the very core of Orthodox Christian theology and of any Orthodox Christian ethics: In Christ we may become what we are called to be from the beginning. Christ is our virtue. The proper ethos of humanity is to form our will to the will of God for us as found in Christ. Meyendorff concludes that

> in "deification" man achieves the supreme goal for which he was created. This goal, already realized in Christ by a unilateral action of God's love, represents both the meaning of human history and a judgment over man. It is open to man's response and free effort (165).

PERICHORESIS

We have noted that for Orthodox Christianity "hypostasis" is not at all reducible to notions of "individuality" or "particular nature." "Hypostasis is the personal 'acting' *source* of natural life; but it is not 'nature' or life itself" (159). Because the two natures of Christ share a common and asymmetrical hypostatic life in the Logos, there is *perichoresis*, a "communication of idioms."

The struggle of Cyril of Alexandria with Nestorius was over the refusal to call Mary the *Theotokos* because God could not have been born of a woman. It also seemed a contradiction to claim that God died on the cross. While this "problem" might be viewed as but another Greek argument over mere words, it is, as Meyendorff notes, fundamentally soteriological. If "death" did not die and Christ is not "born," then how can humanity be said to have been saved from death and born in baptism into a new life? The solution to both of these soteriological concerns is *perichoresis*. In the person of Christ is to be found a union so intimate—but without confusion, since only God can save—that what can be said of the divine can be said of the human.

"En-hypostasized in the Logos," Meyendorff explains, "Christ's humanity, in virtue of the 'communication of idioms,' is penetrated with divine 'energy' " (163–164). The man Jesus is, then, hypostatically God, and there is a *perichoresis* of the divine and the human. This "communication" is, also, available to those "in Christ." To be "in Christ" is union with God, but by grace. So while the notion of *perichoresis* primarily expresses the belief that in Christ hypostatic union allows a communication of characteristics such that it may be said that God was born and that God died, it may also be said that—by grace and the free striving of the human hypostasis—humanity may rise from the dead and sit at the right hand of the Father in Christ. It is the "communication" (perichoretic) of the "immanent" God (who is unchanging *because* he is love) which allows humanity in its nature (an *ousia* made from and for love) to fulfill its call to be divine (perichoretically) by personal "striving" (movement that is "free" or hypostatic) from out of "death" (the consequences of the free choice of turning from God who is our life).

SUMMARY

A virtue ethic as described in these pages involves striving in the direction of one's end, from out of one's beginning. This chapter has presented the elements of that dynamic as Orthodox Christians understand them. It has been an attempt to summarize an Eastern Church response to "where have we come from?" and "where are we going?"

In the development of Eastern Christian thought from Athanasius, to the Cappadocians, and through John Chrysostom to the theologians employed in this chapter, there are to be found certain basic understandings essential to an Orthodox Christian virtue ethic. In combating Arian thought, Athanasius fundamentally shifted the notion of nature that was inherited from Origen. Origen's cosmos is an expression of God's nature, and that nature is characterized by immobility. To distinguish between God and creation, Athanasius described creation as an act of the will of God. God's will is ontologically distinct from the human nature that it brings into existence. It is by nature that the Father generates the Son, but it is by will that human nature comes into being.

Human nature is a willed *ousia*, and, as such, is created to be "open" and "dynamic," insofar as it is from and in need of God as the source and end of being and life. Therefore human nature is characterized in Eastern Christian thought by reference to participation in God. As developed by Maximus the Confessor, "will" is the dynamic aspect of nature—both the nature of God and of humanity. As such, "will" is not a property of person (*hypostasis*) but of nature (*ousia*). According to Maximus, God grants to humanity being, eternal being, goodness, and wisdom. The first two are of the human essence, but the second two are to be gained by volition. He maintains that,

> For this reason he is said to be made "to the image and likeness of God": to the image of his being by our being, to the image of his eternal being by our eternal being (even though not without a beginning, it is yet without end); to the likeness of his goodness by our goodness, to the image of his wisdom by our wisdom. The first is by nature, the second by grace. Every rational nature indeed is made to the image of God; but only those who are good and wise are made to his likeness. [27]

This insistence on the dynamic nature of human nature explains why Maximus required that Christ be said to have two wills—that of God and that of the human nature. In the Trinity there is but one will, because there is one nature.

Salvation is understood as the reversal of the *hypostatic* choice of Adamic humanity. Inasmuch as *hypostasis* indicates the "freedom" of humanity—and is not of nature—it is the possibility to turn from God and corrupt human nature or to turn toward God and fulfill human nature. Jesus—in his life, death, and resurrection—hypostatically reconstitutes humanity as in God, which is the *telos* of human nature. It is *in* this "new humanity," available through Jesus, that we may be freed from the oppression of death by hypostasizing Christ's humanity. Since nature is open to and created for God—a God able to reach hypostatically out of the divine to human nature, while remaining divine—it is possible to "strive for" the virtue or "excellence" of the "theanthropos," the God-human unity in Christ.

Striving or sanctification is the personal, i.e., free or hypostatic, embracing of the grace of the new life in Christ. Church, as understood by Eastern Christians, is the "mystery" or sacrament of that offering and its free acquisition. Maximus the Confessor maintains that "the holy Church of God is an image of God because it realizes the same union of the faithful with God." [28] It is not the locus for mere imitation of Christ, but for *praxis*, "life *in* Christ." It is hypostasized Christification. Since an aspect of nature, as understood by Orthodox Christians, is will—energy, movement, or *thelemata*—that "movement" may be hypostatically directed to the *telos* of *theosis* in Christ; and this is striving. The movement of human nature may also be mutilated in its movement by directing it, again hypostatically, toward loves that are not the end of human nature.

We have then, Orthodox Christianity insists, come from God. We are not a necessary expression of, nor an overflow of that God. We are a free creation coming forth from God's love. We are "other" than God in our freedom; yet as intended to share God's life, we are incomplete without God. There is a call to human completion at the very core of human being. While that "ought" may be dimmed and frustrated, it can never be extinguished. We are created able to freely seek our perfection in God. We are also, as genuinely free, able to seek after what we can never be. We are a created nature fitted for God's grace, God's gift of a shared life. The meaning, therefore, of humanity is to be found in the Logos, the Word which was in the beginning. Christ is God's meaning for humanity, therefore, even from the beginning. In Christ, humanity is renewed to strive after divine likeness in a perfect community of persons.

Creation is not an inferior—merely reflective—aspect of God, inasmuch as it is material. The Creation is a reaching out of God toward humanity. The world, as created, is a mystery of God's gift of love. Humanity is not a mere part or fragment of creation, seeking after wholeness in reunion with it. We are not born of the world, but of God. Creation is, rather, to find its meaning in humanity. The world's "to be" is found in its realization as the gift or mystery of God's love for humanity. Through the lifting up of creation to a renewed sacramental awareness, humanity finds its own salvation as gifted by God for the life of the world. The creation of humanity as male and female is also an opportunity for recovering the mystery of communion, no less than is the monastic life.

There is then in creation a "challenging-goal." It is this irreducible "ought" that humanity must come to terms with. What ought we to be? What narrative will energize that movement? Orthodox Christianity has traditionally presented its "what we ought to be" with an interpretation of the biblical story of the Creation in the "image and likeness" of God. We are, it claims, created in the image of God, and, as free, are called to receive the gift by striving after the likeness. The image of God is to be received as a task to be cultivated.

The nature of the image of God in humanity is, perhaps, best expressed by maintaining that humanity is made up of persons, i.e., that which is able to reach out even beyond nature to the other in self-giving love. We are, as human, dynamic beings; we are always becoming. The question of Orthodox Christianity—and of any virtue ethic—is what do we want to become? The church is the vehicle of that becoming.

As understood by Orthodox Christians, sin in the beginning, and even now, is the refusal of grace. We are free to turn from the gift of God's life for us, but in doing so we bring death into the world. As created in the image and likeness of God, even death and sin cannot destroy the challenging-goal of the deification of humanity. Nothing can ever destroy God's will for us. The biblical story of the Fall is the story of how freedom directed to false ends has transformed the context of human striving, but the more fundamental narrative of the true end of humanity in God's love has not changed.

In Christ, death is no more. In his humanity Christ has personally embraced death, that in his virtue humanity might personally embrace life. Church—as the "new life" in Christ—is believed in, even as Christ is believed in. [29] Church is the mystery of God's love, where God's gift may be received and lived. The resurrected life and its virtues are finely described in *The Ladder* of John Climacus, unraveled in detail in chapter 3. Something equivalent to that description ought to be available for the married life, but is not. If marriage is an ecclesial entity, as is monasticism, for the making of Christians, then it ought to have a discernable movement that is fully equivalent to the celibate vocation. The next chapter will attempt to suggest the shape of just such a virtue ethic for the married life.

Elisabeth Behr-Sigel—a "feminist" Orthodox Christian theologian— maintains that humanity is radically different from the rest of God's creation because of its ability to transcend itself in the direction of God. "The divine Uni-Trinity is the fulness of the communion of different persons," she writes, "the archetype of the restored human communion of which the Church is both the prophetic sign and seed." [30] There is, she contends, a "fundamentally dynamic orientation of human nature as it was intended and created by God" (83). "Anthropos"—Behr-Sigel's preferred usage—in its "nature is not, or rather does not *become* itself, except to the degree that it exists 'in God' or 'in grace' " (83). Therefore, humanity is being "open toward God and is called upon to 'grow in the divine life' according to the mysterious synergy of . . .

created freedom and of the divine Breath" (83). She goes on to assert that there are to be found in the grand vision of the Eastern Fathers some verbal excesses that do not reflect the "fundamental equality of man and woman and their common vocation of deification" (91). This notion of a "common vocation" is, she laments, a "talent" that has been hidden in the ground. She hopes to find in Orthodox Christian thought "a spirit not of petrified traditionalism but of creative faithfulness in the dynamism of the authentic Tradition" (92). In the next chapter, I will try to be creatively faithful to the tradition by uncovering a married asceticism.

Marriage will be shown to be the practice whereby virtue is attained "perichoretically," i.e., by "making room for the other." That "other" is one's "spouse" and, thereby, the "spouse" that is Christ. The "hypostatic communion" which is the "Body of Christ" is the mystery of the church. Natures may hypostatically coinhere, if there is love. God is such love, and humanity is freely called from and for that same Divine Love. While the sharing (*perichoresis*) of divine life is achieved by divinity and not humanity, it still requires striving on the part of humanity. It is the "new creation" accomplished by God and offered as grace, but can be received—as nature's proper orientation—only as free, i.e., as personal choice. Christ's virtue is achieved kenotically, hypostatically "making room for" the other even as he "made room for" (shared or tasted) the death of human nature. An asymmetrical Christology means that for Jesus to "strive" is to pour himself out (*kenosis*), and to experience perichoretically, as God, the death of his creation. Our experience of God is also asymmetrical: It is "perichoretic," and it is striving, a hypostatic divesting of nature—particularly under the aspect of will—to make room for the other.

NOTES

1. Vladimir Lossky (d. 1958) was one of a generation of Russian intellectuals displaced by the revolution. John Meyendorff has called him "one of the best Orthodox Theologians in our time" in Vladimir Lossky, *In the Image and Likeness of God*, ed. John H. Erickson and Thomas E. Bird, with a Foreword by John Meyendorff (New York: St. Vladimir's Seminary Press, 1974), 9.

2. Vladimir Lossky, *Orthodox Theology: An Introduction* (New York: St. Vladimir's Seminary Press, 1978), 51.

3. Georges Florovsky (d. 1979) was one of the "lights" of the postrevolution diaspora of Russian Church intellectuals. He was the first of them to come to America—in 1948—from St. Sergius Orthodox Theological Academy in Paris. He was Dean of St. Vladimir's Seminary, New York, and taught at both Harvard and Princeton. From about the mid-1930s, he was European Orthodoxy's foremost spokesman in the Ecu-

menical movement. See, Andrew Blane, ed., *Georges Florovsky: Russian Intellectual and Orthodox Churchman* (New York: St. Vladimir's Seminary Press, 1993).

4. Georges Florovsky, *The Collected Works of Georges Florovsky*, vol. 3, *Creation and Redemption* (Belmont, Massachusetts: Nordland Publishing Company, 1976), 45.

5. Lossky, *Orthodox Theology*, 55.

6. Ibid., 56.

7. Ibid., 57.

8. Ibid.

9. John Meyendorff, *Byzantine Theology: Historical Trends and Doctrinal Themes* (New York: Fordham University Press, 1979), p. 134.

10. *Orthodox Theology*, 64–65.

11. Ibid., 67.

12. Ibid.

13. Florovsky, *Creation and Redemption*, 73.

14. Meyendorff, *Byzantine Theology*, 140.

15. Gregory Palamas, *Triads*, 1, 1, 9.

16. Georgios I. Mantzarides, *The Deification of Man: St. Gregory Palamas and the Orthodox Tradition*, trans. Liadain Sherrard, (New York: St. Vladimir's Seminary Press, 1984), 16.

17. Ibid., 18–19.

18. Ibid., 21.

19. Ibid., 22.

20. *Orthodox Theology*, 70.

21. *Byzantine Theology*, 138.

22. The "condition" into which all are born is death. This understanding is why Orthodox Christians have such difficulty understanding the "immaculate conception" of Mary—since Adam and Eve's sin is a matter of transmitted death and not of a *macula* or "mark" on human nature.

23. *Byzantine Theology*, 145.

24. Ibid., 146.

25. *Orthodox Theology*, 80.

26. *Byzantine Theology*, 151.

27. *Maximus the Confessor: Selected Writings*, trans. George C. Berthold, *The Classics of Western Spirituality: A Library of the Great Spiritual Masters* (New York: Paulist Press, 1985), 64 (*The Four Hundred Chapters on Love*, Third Century 25).

28. Ibid., 187–88, (*Mystagogy*, chapter 1).

29. It is common for Orthodox Christian theologians to startle others by noting that Orthodox Christians believe in the Church just as they believe in God the Father, Jesus Christ, and the Holy Spirit. When the Creed is recited, they explain, "I *believe* in one holy Catholic and Apostolic Church" means that "Church" is an "object of faith." One cannot *believe* in an institution. The most famous formulation of this assertion is: "The Church of Christ is not an institution; it is a new life with Christ and in Christ, guided by the Holy Spirit." Sergius Bulgakov, *The Orthodox Church* (London: The Centenary Press, 1935), 9.

30. Elisabeth Behr-Sigel, *The Ministry of Women in the Church*, trans. Stephen Bigham (California: Oakwood Publications, 1991), 85.

6

Virtue and Marriage

In homily 13 on First Corinthians, John Chrysostom insists that mere knowledge is not sufficient for the Christian life. Knowledge is a part, but the whole is virtue. [1] Christian life is like the pagan games in that it is a contest for the crown of virtue. It is unlike the games in that all, and not a few, are called to receive the crown. According to Chrysostom, the Apostle Paul likens Christianity to a race and a struggle so "that none may despairingly withdraw from the conflicts in behalf of virtue." [2] Both baptism and Eucharist, according to Chrysostom, require that one show a life worthy of these gifts. He writes that

> if we depart having become nothing better here, even though we repent ever so earnestly there it will do us no good. For it was our duty to strive while yet remaining within the lists, not after the assembly was broken up idly to lament and weep: as that rich man did, bewailing and deploring himself, but to no purpose and in vain, since he overlooked the time in which he ought to have done these things. [3]

As he examines Paul's dealings with the troubled church in Corinth, Chrysostom observes that Paul agrees that they are, indeed, wise, strong, and held in good repute, while he is weak, dishonored, and a fool for the sake of Christ. Having "agreed" with them, according to Chrysostom, Paul asks why any Christian would want to acquire characteristics that are not of Christ? Chrysostom understands Paul to be doing the practical task of asking what sort of excellence or virtue is adequate to the *telos* of life which is found in Christ, and mirrored by Paul and the other Apostles? What virtues supporting the practice of what sort of life would serve to make intelligible the Gospel of God's love for us in Christ? [4]

Chrysostom considers how Paul presents himself as an exemplar of Christian virtue.

> How great is our teacher's boldness of speech! How highly finished the
> image, when he can even exhort others here unto! Not that in self-
> exaltation he doth so, but implying that virtue is an easy thing! [5]

The image of virtue that Paul presents to the Corinthians is one rooted in
the realization that Christ is our truth. Christ is our virtue and, also, the
excellence of God. [6] Chrysostom, explaining how Paul schools the Corinthians,
considers that since they have mocked and derided Paul, they should then
have little trouble taking the next step and imitating him. If the Corinthians
cannot hear Paul, then how are they to listen to Christ? "For the difference
between me and you," Chrysostom has Paul reflect, "is not so great as between
Christ and me: and yet I have imitated him." [7] It is clear that Chrysostom
sees Paul as claiming that the passions displayed by the Corinthians are
maintained only with difficulty, while the virtues displayed by Paul and the
Apostles are "easy" to reconcile with the faith. In any case the difference
between Paul and the Corinthians is a small one, a difference of ends and
not of ability. If Christ is our end, then his virtue is of our true nature.

Chrysostom suggests that Paul be taken to task and his virtue examined
in order to see if it is "easy" and for all to acquire. He will herewith for our
edification produce a sketch of Paul so that we might see God at work in
him. The description will consider from bottom to top the "work of art"
that Paul has become as one would examine a great sculpture. Chrysostom
concludes at the end of his examination that in Paul's life of poverty, dishonor,
and nakedness is to be found a figure of the very crown of virtue which ought
to be desired by all. Thus far, Chrysostom is reenforcing my contention that
virtue and the life of virtue are central and essential to Christianity as understood in the Eastern Church, but that life of virtue would seem to be attained,
if Paul is an example, by way of ascetical denial. In what way is such a life
"easy," i.e., for all? Are all called to abandon the world in holy poverty and
celibate chastity? To answer these questions, the great preacher of Antioch
and Constantinople now turns to his audience of "ordinary" Christians.

IS RENUNCIATION THE ONLY WAY TO CHRISTIAN VIRTUE?

Chrysostom requires that we also enter the contest of virtue in Christ. We
are, all of us, summoned to a contest of virtue, but we are ill-equipped because
we are like fat athletes. We are "fat" with our riches. As "fat," we cannot hope
to enter the "games" and win the "crown." If they are to enter the arena of
virtue, what does John Chrysostom require of his people? One might well
expect him to issue an ascetic's summons to abandon all riches and to enter

a monastery, but, he announces, the problem is not in wealth or in their state in life. "For God made nothing evil but all things very good." [8] They "miss the mark" not in being rich, but in failing to distribute their riches to the poor. There is only God, the end of all of creation. Whether rich or poor, whatever is must be, in its end, for God. The *telos* of everything, to include "riches," is to be found in God.

Although Chrysostom was renown for the asceticism of monastic withdrawal from the world, he also saw a path of Christian virtue that did not travel away from the world and its riches but through it. This is our connection to marriage. There would seem to be two ways to virtue in connection with the world and its riches, virtue may be found *either* in renunciation or in almsgiving. The same possibility seems to hold for marriage and the Christian life in general, either leave the world or find God in it. According to Chrysostom and the Greek Fathers, all is to be sanctified. Both sides of the Christian "coin" of virtue are to be valued, the side of renunciation and the side of generosity. While much has been written in the East on the glories of the celibate life, the other side of the coin, the life of the married Christian, seems to have been treated far less. Since the *telos* of every Christian is *theosis*, one ought to be able to describe the life of Christian virtue as it is found in the richness of marriage. Such is the task of this chapter. As John Chrysostom has written:

> St. Paul tells us to seek peace and the sanctification without which it is impossible to see the Lord. So whether we presently live in virginity, in our first marriage, or in our second, let us pursue holiness, that we may be counted worthy to see Him and to attain the Kingdom. [9]

MARRIAGE, A SCHOOL FOR VIRTUE

Our study of recent and past Orthodox Christianity in the previous chapters revealed a broad consensus that every created person, in every state of life, is called to the *telos* of *theosis*. All are called to become by grace everything that God is by nature. God is free, hence the human person must in freedom cultivate God's gift. God is love, hence the working out of the Christian life is with others. The mapping out of the free human movement toward deification in a monastic community of virtue is amply documented in a work such as *The Ladder of Divine Ascent*, described in chapter 3. Any number of other treatments—less comprehensive but fully illustrative of the centrality of virtue—might have been presented. None of these works, however, would have dealt in the same way and so extensively with marriage as they did with celibate life. There is *nothing* in the tradition concerning marriage that is so extensive, complete, and exhaustive as is, for example, *The Ladder.*

In one of the very few Orthodox Christian works devoted to married life, Paul Evdokimov laments that the two ways of celibate and married asceticism seem to have become alienated from one another. So much of a rupture has occurred that, according to Evdokimov, "we are no longer speaking the same language; it seems that we are in the presence of two worlds that no longer understand each other." [10] Evdokimov intends his words to be a response to the need for an Orthodox Christian description of Nuptial Spirituality. He contends that work in this area must show marriage to be eschatological. Marriage also reaches out for the "eighth day," as does monasticism. "The nuptial marriage-priesthood," Evdokimov writes, "is *ontological,* the new creation that saturates human time with eternity." [11] Marriage, he holds, is fully worthy of study along the lines of a Christian practice that moves the couple toward the summit of deification. We read that "man and woman move toward one another by 'mutually getting to know each other,' by revealing themselves to each other for a shared ascent; nothing comes to ennoble or legitimize, still less to 'pardon' this meaning that royally imposes itself before, or even independent of, procreation." [12] Before it is anything else, then, marriage is a shared ascent. One is fully justified, therefore, in seeking in marriage a "ladder of divine ascent," a way of *theosis.*

My strategy will be to begin with the Orthodox Christian liturgy of marriage. Books are able to bring together and make present what was otherwise scattered. Liturgy is a mode of "bringing together" that, undoubtedly, predates books. Liturgy and books are capable not only of informing but also forming those who "enter" them. What might the liturgy of marriage reveal about the formation of believers? What virtues supporting the practice of what sort of life would serve to make intelligible the story of God's love for creation as rendered there? If, as noted above, baptism and Eucharist require a life worthy of them, then what might marriage require of Christians?

Stanley Harakas, in an article outlining sources for the doing of Orthodox Christian ethics, has written that the marriage service is both a source of and key to Orthodox Christian ethics. [13] As a method for doing ethics, Harakas insists that the Orthodox Christian propensity for presenting liturgical practices is appropriate and "precisely the way which the Orthodox Church embodies and communicates these concerns." [14] Following the method defended by Harakas, I will examine the Orthodox Christian ritual of marriage seeking indications of a virtue ethic. In examining the ritual, I will search for what it can tell us about narrative, *telos,* community, mentoring, practice, and virtue. I will conclude this chapter by considering four nuptial virtues: chastity, humility, obedience, and love. These virtues will be compared to chastity, humility, obedience, and love as rendered in *The Ladder.* First, however, a general description of the ritual of Holy Matrimony will be presented to provide some minimal orientation prior to a more specific analysis.

HOLY MATRIMONY

The sacrament or rite of marriage [15] is composed of two moments connected by a procession. The first moment of the service is the betrothal. The betrothal is followed by a procession accompanied by Psalm 128. The final element is the crowning of the bridal pair.

The betrothal begins when the priest and the couple have assembled in the back of the church. The invocation "Blessed is our God" begins the service, and it is followed by a litany that contains petitions peculiar to this ritual. The blessings invoked for the couple include children, peaceful love, oneness of mind, steadfast faith, a blameless way of life, an honorable marriage, and a bed undefiled (2). The priest chants: "O eternal God ... who didst bless Isaac and Rebecca, and didst make them heirs of Thy promise: Bless also these Thy servants," (3) thus locating the couple in the context of the story of how couples serve God. After a call to bow their heads, the priest prays that the Lord who has espoused the church might so bless and preserve this couple.

The rings are blessed and are exchanged by the couple as a prayer is chanted asking that God—who accompanied the servant of Abraham, in his search for an appropriate spouse, signified by drawing water from a well— might also accompany this couple and fulfill their promise. The nature of that promise is described in the next line as the possibility of being established in a "holy union which is from Thee" (5). God who has brought forth a people "from generation to generation" (5) is called on to fulfill the promise made by this pair, signified by a ring, and to lead them forward. The prayer concludes by likening the pledge of the couple to that of Joseph, Daniel, and Tamar. The ring, placed on the right hand in the Eastern tradition, is likened to the ring placed on the prodigal son when he returned to his father. The right hand of Moses was armed by the might of God in the passage through the sea, the prayer continues, so also might the strength of this couple be found in God. The prayer concludes by asking that God's "angel go before them all the days of their life" (5–6).

Having concluded the betrothal in the back of the church, the wedding party goes in procession to the church proper accompanied by the singing of Psalm 128. Evdokimov notes that this psalm has been part of the service since the fourth century, and it clearly establishes the eschatological direction of marriage. "The espousals on earth," he contends, "are the beginning of the ascension of Zion in the Taboric light." [16] Meyendorff, similarly, interprets the procession to be an "entrance into the Kingdom of Christ: the marriage contract concluded through the betrothal service will now be transformed." [17]

The next movement in the marriage ritual begins with the exclamation "Blessed is the Kingdom." [18] The litany that follows is little different from that of the betrothal, except that "fruitfulness" is now stressed. Fruitfulness is to flow from marriage by way of God's blessing, the prayer proclaims, as it did at the marriage in Cana. The "harvest" of marriage, as expressed in the litany, is to include chastity, children, and a blameless life.

Three long prayers follow the litany and precede the placing of crowns on the couple. The first prayer asks that God who is the author of all, and who blessed Adam and Eve, bless and be present to this couple. God is called on to bless them as he did Abraham and Sarah, Isaac and Rebecca, Jacob and Rachel, Joseph and Aseneth, and Zechariah and Elizabeth. As he crowned those marriages, so also grant this couple "a peaceful life, length of days, chastity, mutual love in the bond of peace, long-lived offspring, gratitude from their children, a crown of glory that does not fade away" (11). The prayer continues by asking that the abode of this couple be filled with good things, "so that they may give in turn to those in need" (11).

The second prayer begins much as the first, but it continues with the theme of obedience. The two are to be subject to one another, the petition declares, and so be blessed as were Abraham and Sarah, and the others as in the first prayer. This prayer links being subject to one another with being "preserved." God is called upon to preserve this couple as he did Noah, Jonah, and the three holy children. The prayer describes this preservation, found in obedience to one another, as the will of God that results in a "gladness" of the sort given to the Empress Helen when she found the true cross. The cross, which brings the joy found only in obedience, is next associated with martyrdom. The priest prays that God who remembers "martyrs" ("witnesses," in Greek) remember the parents of this couple, and the attending friends. Images of the Kingdom fulfilled are woven together with nuptial signs of fruitfulness as the way in which God remembers the bridal pair. The "fruit" of their bodies is associated with the "fruit" of the Kingdom. Their harvest is to be a "luxuriant vine" and "full ears of grain" (14). The bridal couple are central to the "remembrance" of the fruitfulness of the Kingdom. It is a Kingdom which is yet to come, but is already "remembered" in their union. It is this harvest of the Kingdom that is described as finding favor in

God's sight, making the man and the woman to "shine like the stars of heaven" (14).

The final prayer before the crowning revisits the creation of the first man and woman. The prayer asks that this marriage might be fulfilled as a recreation of what God willed to create in the beginning. Today, in the prayer, God is again stretching forth his hands in creation. Once more, today, man and woman are called by God to be the crown of his work. Once more the blessing is offered.

The crowns are bestowed on the couple and two Scripture readings follow: Ephesians 5.20–33 and John 2.1–11. The first reading likens nuptial love to that of Christ for the church; the second reading is the story of the marriage in Cana of Galilee. The prayer that follows declares the pericope to be evidence that marriage is honorable and that it ought to result in chastity and walking in God's ways (20). The Lord's Prayer and the sharing of a cup of blessed wine come next. These elements are, no doubt, remnants of when the ritual was more firmly established in the eucharistic liturgy. The rite of crowning was not separated from the eucharistic liturgy until the tenth century. [19]

A ritual dance is now executed by the nuptial pair guided by the priest. While circling the center of the church, three times, three verses are sung. First, a verse is sung announcing that Isaiah might now rejoice because Emmanuel is born. As the procession continues, a second verse praises "martyrs" (witnesses) who have fought the good fight and received their crowns. [20] Lastly, Christ is glorified as the one who is "the apostles' boast, the Martyrs' joy whose preaching was the consubstantial Trinity." [21] If the three prayers before the crowning establish the context of Christian marriage as eschatological, i.e., that the "crown" of creation is God's will and that God's will is that the human pair, even from Adam and Eve, is called by God to be the crowning glory of his love, then the requirements for such a journey (or "dance") are announced in the three short verses that attend the dance. Marriage can participate in the recreation of the world, as a foretaste of the Kingdom, if Isaiah's hope was fulfilled and the Messiah has come, if we will witness to this love in our marriage, and if the Messiah who has come and of whom we witness is himself communion with God in a Trinity of love.

The crowns are ritually removed after the dance. The bridegroom is promised a crown of victory in witnessing to Christ, if like Abraham, Isaac, and Jacob he walks in God's peace and keeps his ways of righteousness. The bride is called on to find her crown as did Sarah, Rebecca, and Rachel by being pleasing to God. A final exhortation asks for God's blessing that the promise of this couple be fulfilled in the Kingdom.

NARRATIVE, TELOS, COMMUNITY, MENTORING, PRACTICE, AND VIRTUE

In this section I will consider what the ritual just described in general terms can more specifically reveal about narrative, *telos*, community, and mentoring. Each element will contribute to the uncovering of the practice that will lead to the *telos* of *theosis*, and its attendant virtues. The story that is told by the ritual is composed of many strands of scriptural material that is alluded to and then woven into a rich tapestry celebrated in a service that might be sung in little over one hour.

As noted above, the service begins with the couple and priest gathered in the back of the church in a formal betrothal. After the rings are exchanged, the priest prays that the pledge of the couple be like the pledge of Joseph, Daniel, and Tamar. The scriptural narratives of Joseph, Daniel, and Tamar evoked in the wedding ritual are alike in that they contain descriptions of the ambiguities of sexual expression and of how pledging faith in God can transform even misdirected loves.

The story of Joseph's life in Egypt begins with the passion of Potiphar's wife for Joseph. The imprisonment of Joseph is a result of this passion, but it finds its transformation and completion in the ring awarded by Pharaoh. [22] At the beginning of the Daniel sagas, we find Daniel pledging that he will not defile himself in the court of the King. As in the story of Joseph, Daniel's faithfulness leads to being honored by the King. [23] His pledge to honor God leads us to the story of Susanna. It is another narration of how passions can destroy. [24] The story of Tamar, which interrupts the biblical story of Joseph, is the story of a Canaanite woman who is given in succession to the sons of Judah, only to have them die. In her search after righteousness, Tamar encounters Judah, and as a sacred prostitute she secures his ring, a pledge that will identify him as one who is in her debt. Judah, unable to retrieve his pledge, is told that Tamar is pregnant. Judah is prepared to condemn Tamar, but at the climax of the story she produces his pledge. Tamar is vindicated and Judah is transformed, seeing himself as guilty before God. [25] All of these familiar stories involve sexuality and passion both gone astray and redeemed. In all of the narratives we also see passion ending in God's will, often in spite of the actors.

The invocation of Joseph, Daniel, and Tamar is preceded by mention of Abraham and the story of his search for an appropriate spouse for his son. Specific mention is made of the sign that Abraham's servant drew water from the well. The narratives invoked after mention of Joseph, Daniel, and Tamar are those of Moses' passage through the sea and the story of the prodigal son.

The text leads us to consider the ring, which is traditionally placed on the right hand, as finding its meaning in both the story of an exodus and in the story of a return, thus is sexuality not condemned but contextualized. Married sexuality is understood here as a way to participate in the journey toward freedom from all that obstructs the intended return to God.

The wedding party moves to the center of the church accompanied by the festive responsorial singing of Psalm 128. Considered as a brief narrative, this psalm begins by declaring as blessed all who reverence God and walk in his ways. The second through fourth verses describe a fruitful married existence. The last verses relate the fruitfulness of a happy marriage to the fruitfulness of the Kingdom. It is noteworthy that the prayer before the procession begins mentions attending angels. The narratives of the procession are clearly eschatological. The Orthodox Christian ritual of marriage contains the promise of a "realized eschatology." Marriage is to be no less "eucharistic," than the eucharistic breaking of bread.

The narrative of eschatological fruitfulness is continued in the part of the service called the crowning. While the finding of water at a well by Abraham's servant set the narrative context at the beginning of the service (the betrothal), at this point the context for the stories to be told is set by the story of water being changed into wine by Jesus at a marriage.

The three long prayers that precede the crowning begin by calling to mind the story of Adam and Eve, who were blessed to be the crown of God's good creation. There is no indication given that sexuality might constitute a fall of any sort. Rather, Adam and Eve are said to have been blessed by God. Other blessed couples are now drawn into the marriage service. The stories of Abraham, Sarah, Isaac, Rebecca, Jacob, Rachel, Joseph, Aseneth, Zechariah, and Elizabeth are all included as stories of couples blessed by God. The prayer draws our attention to a specific aspect of their narratives. All of these couples are blessed by the virtue of generosity. In learning to give to one another, they are prepared to entertain God.

The second prayer again calls up the narratives of those mentioned above, but this time we are led to attend to their being obedient to one another, which, in this section, is declared to be the blessing bestowed. These stories of couples blessed to learn generosity through subjecting themselves to one another are in stark contrast to those constituted by the narratives of subjecting another to one's passions, as related in the stories of Joseph, Daniel, and Tamar evoked at the betrothal.

All of these narratives are woven together by the ritual's call to consider the stories of Noah, Jonah, and the three children associated with the story of Daniel. These are stories, the marriage ritual claims, of God's preservation.

If the narratives describe the sort of preservation that might be expected of Christian marriage, then it is not one of untroubled romantic bliss. The narratives of Noah, Jonah, and the three young men in the furnace of Nebuchadnezzar tell of a "preservation" that entails extraordinary trial.

If there is any doubt that the ritual is calling elements of trial and struggle to our attention in these narratives, the next story eliminates any confusion. Not a story from the Bible, but a story from Byzantine history is evoked. We are asked to consider how the Empress Helen found the true cross. This is the sort of "gladness" that is being pointed to in the narratives of preservation. This reference to the story of St. Helen, according to John Meyendorff, "points to *the cross* as a way of kingship, as the center of the mystery of salvation and, therefore, also as the center of the mystery of marriage." [26]

The final prayer before the couple is crowned returns to the story of Adam and Eve. The story of the Creation is evoked as if it were still at the beginning. The narratives are to be read, therefore, as the story of what might still be. If the betrothal narratives placed marriage in the context of God's story of love for humanity and warned that "mere" sexuality is not the end of human love—just as not wealth as such but generosity is the end of human resourcefulness—then the narratives of the crowning place marriage within stories of God's "shelter." The "shelter" of marriage is presented not as a static or private escape from the world, but, rather, as an "ark" that preserves marriage for its intended resurrection. Although marriage is likened to a fiery furnace, the couple will be preserved if their hope is in God. Marriage is to be, then, not a static escape, but a dynamic vehicle of transfiguration.

Ephesians 5.20–33 and John 2.1–11 are both narratives that continue to display marriage as a story involving becoming like Jesus in his love. It is a blessed change from water into wine. The crown and summit of creation is God's calling forth creatures like himself; beings with the nature to be divine but the freedom to say no. The crown of marriage is to fulfill God's will and to say yes.

During the circular dance that speaks of an eternal procession into God's love, the ritual calls upon those gathered to remember Isaiah's hope, all of the stories of the martyrs, and the "story" of trinitarian love being worked out in us in the person of Christ. Narrative is essential in marriage, as elsewhere, because, as Chrysostom had already observed seventeen hundred years ago, the virtue of a person "cannot be shown without acting." [27] All of the narratives of the marriage ritual assemble and display men and women being transformed, i.e., following after God in freedom and in love, with no necessary impediment because they are married.

The life of the Trinity is a life of free interpersonal love. All of the narratives noted above are stories of people—in and out of marriage—who are personally striving after the *telos* of loving with God's own love. The end of marriage cannot but be the same as is the *telos* of a celibate monk or nun. The difference is practical—*how* to attain the likeness to God that is the calling of all of humanity—not teleological. Meyendorff writes that "marriage and celibacy, if they presuppose different practical behaviors, are based on the same theology of the Kingdom of God and, therefore, on the same spirituality." [28] What is that spirituality? It is the transformation of the human person toward the likeness of God. "Christian marriage," Meyendorff continues, "consists in transforming and transfiguring a natural human affection between a man and a woman into an eternal bond of love, which cannot be broken even by death." [29]

The ritual of marriage is replete with indications of the *telos* of "new life." The betrothal portion in the back of the church begins with the invocation "Blessed is our God," while, by contrast, the service of crowning that begins after the procession to the middle of the church begins with the eucharistic invocation "Blessed is the Kingdom." The betrothal service is informed by a passage that reflects on water, while the crowning is informed by a narrative of changing water into wine. In connection with marriage, according to Meyendorff, "the change of water into wine . . . points to a transfiguration of the old into the new, a passage from death to life." [30] Rebecca's drawing water from the well is but a beginning, as is this moment in the marriage, Meyendorff maintains, but the ultimate *telos* is always the same for this bride or Rebecca. [31] Marriage is a "type" that is realized in the "antitype" of God's love for creation. Marriage, indeed all of creation, finds that it is but a beginning until its meaning is realized in the *telos* toward which it must grow until its fulfillment. Even Christ is a "type" fulfilled in the "antitype" of becoming communion for us. [32] Therefore as all of the stories of the service find their meaning in the *telos* of transformation toward God's likeness, so must this marriage. If our age tends to look at relationships in terms of cause and effect—thus, it would seem, eliminating any teleological considerations— Orthodox Christianity sees purpose or end as the very heart of marriage.

The community of marriage is essentially the same as that of any Orthodox Christian, i.e., the church. The mentors of marriage are, again, essentially those who know the way, whether married or not. When the entire ritual is examined, the community revealed is one that fully appreciates the body and the physical world. It is almost a distortion to express it in this way, because it is difficult to see in the ritual a point where spirituality and materiality diverge. In Christ, all is one. For the community of this ritual, sexuality is no more evil in itself than are abundant riches. Clearly, the Orthodox Christian community here reveals itself as unacquainted with the notion that sexuality associates naturally with corruption.

Meaning is found not primarily in a beginning to be sustained, but in a *telos* to be realized. The community of the liturgy of marriage described in this chapter is a community of exodus and return. The rings of marriage are to be understood, among other things, as a source of strength for the journey out of bondage to anything not of God. Marriage is for the prodigal a way of return to the Father's house. It is a community that is yet on the way, and in the process of answering God's call of transcendent love. Nuptial love is for this community a way—if not *the* way—of return to the love with which God has loved us.

The community of the marriage ritual is one that seeks for chastity (*sophrosyne*) or single-mindedness more than it seeks after mere singleness. Evdokimov goes so far as to consider marriage as more fundamental to the Orthodox Christian community than is monasticism. Not monasticism, but marriage is the most essential icon of the Orthodox Christian faith. He notes that it is monasticism that has need of nuptial symbolism ("betrothed" and "spouse"). "Marriage," according to Evdokimov, "includes within itself the monastic state." [33]

While an Orthodox Christian theologian as well-respected as Paul Evdokimov may insist that marriage is prior to monasticism as an ascetic mode to God, monastics are most often the sought after mentors of the pious in the Orthodox Christian Church. Surely this is not inappropriate inasmuch as the very *telos* of marriage is the same as monasticism. However, the marriage service itself calls on the parents, the friends, and witnesses of the couple to serve as mentors to them. In one of the prayers before the crowning, after calling attention to martyrs, the text asks that the parents participate in this "remembrance" because parents nurture and "make firm the foundations of houses." [34] The service continues by describing the friends of the bridal pair as having been assembled in the same joy. That "joy" was just described in the service as proceeding from a cross. The text requires that those nearest the couple hold them to the descriptions of marriage that have just been given, and who better than those who are experienced in just this sort of nuptial asceticism? There are, however, no such mentors usually recognized in the Orthodox Christian community. Although this absence would seem to constitute a considerable disadvantage to Orthodox Christian couples, it is at least essential that those within the community who do serve as mentors should grasp the appropriate narratives intended to form marriage. The danger is that marriage may come to be seen—if it has not been already—as a form of life that is inferior to celibacy, and thus to secularize it. It would, however, seem appropriate to establish experienced married couples as mentors, which is not now the case. This is, no doubt, due to the perception that celibate spirituality is the primary form of Orthodox Christian asceticism. It is good to be dedicated to God ("chaste"), but such chastity is, fundamentally, dedication to a nuptial love whether one is married or single.

It is clear that the ritual assumes a community much more familiar with the narratives of the Bible than are the Orthodox Christians of America. The story of marriage as finding its end in God's love is constructed by the weaving together of a great many stories that are simply alluded to and then placed in dialogue with other complex narratives. To "hear" the story being told in the ritual requires a listener not just familiar but thoroughly formed by a community grounded in Scripture.

The marriage liturgy is the memory of and participation in the gift of the new creation. Again one comes to the question: What practice supported by what virtues will attain to the *telos* of *theosis*? The answer is that marriage first must be practiced not as "private" but, as Vigen Guroian has put it, as an essentially "ecclesial reality," [35] i.e., within the community of the church and her narratives, seeking the end of deification. Marriage as envisioned here is never private, but, rather, the concern of all of the Christian community.

Practice here is understood as the congruence of liturgy and life. If liturgy has been engaged in this way—and not as a mere accompaniment to the couple's private intentions—then it is capable of an "effect." As described by Zizioulas, one who is open to liturgy "gets into the habit of placing himself, his works and history itself under the light and the judgement of the Kingdom, always and in everything seeking its *ultimate* meaning." [36] In liturgy what is discovered "is not a flight or deliverance from space and time or from history, but the biblical perspective of the *transformation* of space and time, as indeed of all the Creation which God's love made 'very good.' " [37] Marriage holds the possibility as practice to be the intersection of the human and the divine, both nuptial affairs.

When married life is practiced as congruent with the marriage rite and its narratives, then it cannot be imagined, as it often is, as that which begins full and then runs toward inevitable depletion. The practice of marriage that is imagined as an ever-decreasing resource would call for skills other than those displayed and celebrated in the Orthodox Christian ritual. Skill in negotiating a return on inevitable failure and consequent self-reliance would be developed and required, if nuptial love is understood as an affection that mysteriously comes and, just as mysteriously, goes.

Preparation for marriage as celebrated by Orthodox Christians would preclude the practice of making sexual activity the end of relationships. There is no indication that marriage is understood in the ritual as part of a right to sexual expression. The context of marriage is not consenting adults, but the church community and its ends. Those involved in, for example, educational institutions that encourage campuses where cohabitation is casual would be forming people with skills appropriate to love if, and only if, love is an exercise in sustaining the initial excitement of ever new sexual expression. Skills and abilities much different from those called for in the Orthodox Christian ritual are taught by men and women to men and women when coital activity is identified as or presumed to be the end of personal relationships. It is difficult to imagine how a male or female "schooled" in a community where coital activity is an end in itself would be able to practice marriage as presented in the Orthodox Christian rite. As analyzed by Evdokimov,

> Public life is invaded by an obsessive and tiresome sexuality. Even the conventions of specialists speak no longer either of love or of Eros, but of sexuality. We are watching its rising tide. [38]

Western culture presently considers sexuality, Evdokimov concludes, as "anatomy delivered to a morbid curiosity, quickly sated." [39]

Since marriage, to include the dimension of sexuality, is an ecclesial affair intended to form Christians in Christlike love, Chrysostom holds that a woman (or, presumably, a man) when she does not meet the demands of the flesh cannot be rejected. Christ loves us, Chrysostom notes, even when we are unavailable and repulsive. [40] If we have not learned to be chaste or single-minded in pursuing the good of a given man or woman, then how can we ever expect to gain victory in the arena for the pursuit of *theosis*?

If we have not learned to be single-minded in pursuing the good of a given man or woman in the practice of Christian marriage, then how can we be crowned victors in the love of God? Referring to the beginning of this chapter, Chrysostom might well have claimed that this is also a sort of "fat" athlete. One formed in relationships that culminate only in convenient sexual expression is hardly prepared for the struggle that marriage entails as described by the marriage liturgy. Again as with wealth, the problem is not with sexual expression as such but with its *telos*.

Marriage is "crowned" to be the practice of the new creation in Christ. God is victorious when creation fulfills the promise of his love. We are victors (crowned) when the practice of God's love as rendered in marriage is fulfilled in us. The crown of God's creation is nothing other than woman and man, together, loving with God's own love. The practice of finding God's love in marriage will involve chastity, obedience, and humility. It will involve effort because "a sacrament *is not magic.*" [41] The ritual of marriage displays the way in which man and woman by participating in Christ, having been freed from death and sin, might grow in the direction of life's end. The practice must be received and lived. According to John Meyendorff:

> The Holy Spirit does not suppress human freedom but, rather, liberates man from the limitations of sinfulness. In the new life, the impossible becomes truly possible, if only man freely accepts what God gives. This applies to marriage as well. [42]

The "crown" of the practice of marriage is victory over "passion," over any "love" that cannot be the proper end of human life. Chastity is clearly—and, perhaps, surprisingly—the foremost virtue of marriage as displayed in the ritual, but all of life and not just sex is to be chaste. "Chastity" is the "mindful" or even "sane" pursuit of the divine. Chastity is not to be conceived merely as the avoidance of sexual activity by the unmarried. "The married as well as the monastic state are two forms of chastity, each one appropriate to its own mode of being." [43] Marriage, according to the ritual, is a practice requiring chastity, i.e., the mindful pursuit of the end of *theosis* for the woman and for the man.

The virtue of chastity is not exercised in the suppression of sexuality, but in the practice of Christian marriage where the end is a new being in Christ. Sexual differentiation, as imagined here, is not the result of a fall from grace but the very will of God and a blessing (161). God is the blessing of marriage and its eschatological fruit. The fruit of married intercourse is, then, no less than God—just as the fruit of riches is God, when one gives to the poor as a child of God rendering oneself incapable of any other way of being. It is a violation of chastity when marriage—or money—is received as its own end, thus desacralizing it. A priestly people practice in chastity the return of all of creation to its proper being as a grace or gift of God. "It is not 'in spite of marriage,' but in its fulfillment," according to Evdokimov, "that spouses live the supernatural and holiness of their union" (163). Therefore in the pursuit of virtue, i.e., asceticism, "chastity stands as the beginning . . . of an integral Christian humanism, turned toward the End" (168).

After attending to preliminary explanations, it is now clear that "the concept of chastity, *sophrosyne,* points out above all a spiritual quality, complete 'knowledge,' the power of the integrity and of the integration of all the elements of life" (168–169). It is the practiced and practical virtue of orientation toward the *telos* of creation. Sex is saved in marriage, and in monasticism, by being reoriented from being its own meaning to being again a gift of God's presence in the flesh. It would not be extreme to say that the Orthodox Christian rite of matrimony recalls sexuality as communion. This is an epicletic movement of offering what is God's back to God in Christ.

Marriage, therefore, cannot be reduced to mere genitality, nor even to reproductive necessity, because it is called to be communion in God and, thus, to give birth to the Spirit. Chastity is the virtue of a priest. As understood by Orthodox Christianity, *all* are called in Christ to be priests. Chastity is, then, the recapitulation of creation. Such a love, according to John Chrysostom, fulfills and transforms what is fallen. We are, he maintains, not simply called to love, but to follow after love. He concludes that "if we are virtuous, love will not perish, for virtue springs from love, and love from virtue." [44]

When the virtue of chastity in the rite of marriage is compared with the classic monastic text of John Climacus, then a profound congruence is uncovered in the apparent difference. There is much indeed in *The Ladder* that seems to identify chastity with the mere avoidance of women, but upon closer examination, chastity is seen to be not a virtue of avoidance but one of engagement. There is an understanding and experience of chastity, in both John Climacus and the Orthodox Christian vision of marriage as seen by Evdokimov, that displays a way of life where sexuality as such causes not "the slightest decline of the inner life." [45] Chastity as described by John Climacus is a virtue that might just as well apply to a married woman or man, although he is addressing monastics.

In *The Ladder* there is a story presented in the section on chastity that qualifies its meaning. John Climacus tells of one—in this case a celibate monk—who comes upon a woman who is naked. The monk in this story, a paragon of virtue, does not flee the nakedness of the other, but is moved to tears and praises God. Evidently when chastity is present, one is neither endangered nor compromised by another's nakedness, but, as in the story told by John Climacus, one is able to find a place of transcendence in a "nakedness" that reaches out toward the Kingdom invoking its fulfillment. He concludes that one such as described in the story would properly be said to be in this life "already risen from the dead." [46] Sagely, he observes "how something that could have brought low one person managed to be the cause of a heavenly crown for another" (179). It is pertinent to our understanding of the virtue of chastity that it is—both for the monastic and the married—the "nakedness" of the other seen as for God that results in a "crown," an eschatological victory.

John Climacus maintains in the same place that the chaste person is not simply one who has never been actively sexual, but someone who has learned to subject everything to the spirit. Chastity is, then, for the married or for the monastic the very reverse of adultery. "Chastity is," therefore, "a name common to all virtues," (172) and is as essential to the monk as to the married. "Chastity," we discover in *The Ladder* and in the marriage liturgy, "makes us familiar with God and as like Him as any man may be" (176). Man, woman, monk, or nun, chastity is an essential virtue as grasped by Orthodox Christianity. There are differences between chastity as displayed and exercised by the marriage rite and in *The Ladder*, but the similarities are far more striking and profoundly essential than are the differences.

One may, of course, fall while chastity is being sought. This virtue is attained only with difficulty in either practice. Falling from chastity seems almost as important in *The Ladder* as attaining it. In *The Ladder*, we read that some seem to come to a sort of chastity with ease. These are those who are in some sense "impotent" by nature, but who still long for some end other than God and, thus, for corruption. As for John Climacus, his "praise goes out each day to those who take the knife, so to speak, to their own evil thoughts" (173). Chastity is not gained at one's ease or without real struggle, according to *The Ladder*, but out of the struggle with failure there can emerge not only chastity but another virtue. That virtue is humility. Humility is also seen as emerging from out of the struggle for chastity in the practice of marriage.

If marriage is, as has been indicated, the practice of pursuing the end of deification in Christ, and if this end requires the virtue of chastity as previously described, then of necessity the virtue of humility will emerge. Humility is in John Climacus the virtue by which celibates recognize that they cannot be their own end. Humility is hard won and often the result of a failure to be chaste. Marriage offers the opportunity to discover that in one's failure to chastely see the other as for God, the truth of one's idolatry of self may be exposed. John Chrysostom offers no end of examples of spouses using one another for their own ends. He also exposes such strategies as pointless, as without a sufficient end.

He notes that it may be the case that a woman is fond of ornament, but a husband is revealed as idolizing himself who uses his wife as his "own proper ornament." [47] A husband who fails to see God as the proper *telos* of a woman is somehow fundamentally responsible for the disorientation of the marriage. When a man or woman is directed by how much the spouse serves to ornament his or her own self, then "beauty" becomes its own end. When this fragile and false beauty fails, so does the marriage. John Chrysostom seems intent on destroying the sense of superiority that enables males to avoid seeing the sins that they report in women as grounded in themselves. And of course this is the point of marriage as an ecclesial entity, i.e., it is not for finding fault with the other, but for reaching out in Christlike love in order to transform the self. One ought not to do anything that does not benefit the practice. "Tell me," Chrysostom asks, "will the shoemaker ever busy himself about anything which does not belong to or *befit* his trade?" [48]

In *The Ladder* the spiritual friend is of great value in gaining humility. John Climacus writes that

> because of our unwillingness to humble ourselves, God has arranged that no one can see his own faults as clearly as his neighbor does. Hence our obligation to be grateful not to ourselves but to our neighbor and to God for our healing. [49]

This cross reference to *The Ladder* helps make clear why John Chrysostom sees the husband's proud use of his wife as a decoration for himself as contributing fundamentally to the failure of the woman to recognize that she is not to be bejeweled by gold but by virtue. The answer is that in failing to gain humility, the husband also fails to be the kind of "neighbor" or "friend" capable of gracing his spouse with a vision of her own proper end. To see one's spouse as decoration for one's self is to disfigure that person. One is never so disfigured as when one is stripped of virtue. [50] To reach out to the other for the other's good is to acquire a divine likeness. "God is fulness," Evdokimov maintains, "not for Himself, but for his creation." [51] Humility in marriage also requires a transcending of the self toward God in the other in nuptial obedience, which is the very configuration of Christ. [52]

"*Obedience* to God," Evdokimov explains, "supplants all self-sufficiency, every ascendance coming from the world." [53] Only obedience to God is able to support the sort of marriage that does not rest on ends that must fail. Obedience to God is learned in obedience to one another. The marriage ritual calls for some firmer foundation than what each spouse might desire from the other. Not what any one of the two may want, but obedience to what God wills for the other unites marriage, as presented in the Orthodox Christian ritual.

Obedience to God unburdens marriage of the unbearable requirements of modernity. As described by the narratives of popular culture, marriage must serve and meet all of a spouse's needs. In explaining the marriage service, the "Mystery of Love," Alexander Schmemann insists that a marriage that is not ordered to a trinity of man, woman, and active unselfish obedience to God is not a Christian marriage at all. "A marriage," he insists, "which does not constantly crucify its own selfishness and self-sufficiency, which does not 'die to itself' that it may point beyond itself, is not a Christian marriage." [54] Obedience to God results not in the satisfaction of oneself as the center of marriage, but in a cross. The true "sin" of marriage, where it "misses the mark," is not in adultery or in the failure to adjust to the other, according to Schmemann. The real sin of contemporary descriptions of marriage lies in

> the idolization of the family itself, the refusal to understand marriage as directed toward the Kingdom of God. This is expressed in the sentiment that one would "do anything" for his family. . . . The family has here ceased to be for the glory of God; it has ceased to be a sacramental entrance into His presence. It is not the lack of respect for the family, it is the idolization of the family that breaks the modern family so easily, making divorce its almost natural shadow. [55]

Schmemann insists that so long as marriage is seen as solely the concern of those being married, as about them and their wants, and not as something that happens to the church and, so, to creation, then we will never understand marriage as the great mystery. [56] Schmemann thus locates the "problem" of marriage in obedience.

When *The Ladder* is turned to, celibate obedience is revealed as "renunciation of our own life." [57] John Climacus describes the virtue of obedience in terms that would just as well suit Schmemann's description of the virtue of obedience in marriage as disclosed by the ritual. Obedience is when with humility "we resolve to bend the neck and entrust ourselves to another in the Lord." [58] John Climacus holds that without obedience one cannot possibly navigate life, because without obedience one is liable to mistake "the sailor for the helmsman. . . , the sea for the harbor—with the resulting shipwreck." [59] This description, while intended for celibates, would as well suit nuptial navigation. If the primary navigational "virtue" of contemporary marriage is knowing what you want and getting it from the spouse, then the inevitable failure of any such spouse to "give me everything I ever wanted" will soon result in a failure caused by demanding an impossible obedience.

The passage on obedience ends in *The Ladder* where the celibate community of obedience is described as like a furnace. The marriage ritual describes the nuptial pair as being preserved by God even as God preserved the three holy children in Nebuchadnezzar's furnace. [60] In a further parallel, *The Ladder* describes such a community as where one might become "like trees swayed by the wind and driving their roots deeper into the ground, those who live in obedience become strong and unshakable souls." [61] The harvest of married and celibate asceticism is revealed to be the same. Asceticism is required because in marriage or celibate life love is a birthing. The virtues of chastity, obedience, and humility are necessary to allow the "birth" of love that does not come and go, but endures. What is the nature of this love?

At the very beginning of the marriage ritual, the community blesses the promise of betrothal and continues by praying for what the pair need but do not possess. The prayer asks that through this union God "will send down upon them perfect and peaceful love." [62] Such a love is, as the petitions that follow make clear, made present in "oneness of mind," "steadfast faith," a "blameless life," and a "bed undefiled." [63] This is the description of an ascetic journey which the liturgy promises will culminate in deliverance from any "necessity." [64] The "necessity" noted in the litany is not merely freedom from "need," but freedom from fate and chance, from any determination. Married love is the very vehicle which shows the way into a Divine Love that frees us from all that holds us captive, from any and all determination.

The last petition of the service prays that this couple might "progress in life and faith," and so may they be "worthy to enjoy the good things of the promise." [65] Divine Love is, as displayed by the ritual, a personal reaching out for the other. It is a love that is undefiled, blameless, steadfast, and one. It is God reaching out to them, and it is known by their reaching out to one another in a like manner. This is the summit of the marriage journey of discovery, and it is identical, except for the practice, to the virtue of love as it is described by John Climacus in *The Ladder*. At the very "top" of the ladder there is to be found love, and it is "a resemblance to God, insofar as this is humanly possible." [66] Marriage and sanctified celibacy carry us into the same assembly, the same fellowship, the fellowship of virtue in God's love.

This is not a love bound or determined by the flesh. Orthodox Christians do not maintain that marriage is sundered by death, but that its way endures as an aspect of eternity. As Schmemann notes, the promise sought in the Mystery of Marriage "is not taken 'until death parts,' but until death unites us completely." [67] Love is described in *The Ladder* in similar fashion as having "no boundary, and both in the present and in the future age we will never cease to progress in it, as we add light to light." [68]

While the virtue of love maintains different Christian practices, it is the same love. In *The Ladder*, we read that

> someone truly in love keeps before his mind's eye the face of the beloved and embraces it there tenderly. Even during sleep the longing continues

unappeased, and he murmurs to his beloved. That is how it is for the body. And that is how it is for the spirit. [69]

A further congruence may be seen in love's maturation. Schmemann describes the ripening of married love in this way:

> But once, in the light and warmth of an autumn afternoon, this writer saw on the bench of a public square, in a poor Parisian suburb, an old and poor couple. They were sitting hand in hand, in silence, enjoying the pale light, the last warmth of the season. In silence: all words had been said, all passion exhausted, all storms at peace. The whole life was behind—yet all of it was now *present*, in this light, in this warmth, in this silent unity of hands. Present—and ready for eternity, ripe for joy. This to me remains the vision of marriage, of its heavenly beauty. [70]

The mature celibate as described in *The Ladder* comes at the end of his struggles for virtue to a similar quiet, a "*hesychia*." As described by John Climacus, "He who has achieved stillness has arrived at the very center of the mysteries, but he would never have reached these deaths if he had not first seen and heard the sound of waves. . . , if he had not been splashed by those waves." [71] Mere eroticism may fuel a liaison, but only the love found in chastity, humility, and obedience can form a person for *hesychia*, marital or monastic.

SUMMARY

Marriage in the Orthodox Christian Church, as described in this chapter, is a practice whereby the likeness to God in love, the human *telos*, is sought. Marriage is no less a vocation than is sanctified celibacy. Both marriage and holy celibacy aim at union in the love with which God has loved the world. Marriage as a Christian ascetical practice, i.e., as a way of life, is the path on which the chaste find the love of God through and in one another in obedience and humility.

We see that there are no "ordinary" Christians by virtue of involvement in the "flesh," and that all are called to virtue in the Orthodox Christian fellowship. No one is exempt from entering the arena of virtue. The practices for winning the crown of virtue will, indeed, vary, but the goal is the same. Orthodox Christians have here the basic elements for the charting of a fundamental topology of virtue. For example "chastity," seemingly different for the celibate and the married Christian, is revealed to be essentially the same for both. *Sophrosyne* is single-minded attention to the end of deification, God's will for the other and for oneself.

Our work has, then, uncovered among other things a basic Orthodox Christian topology of virtue in the analysis of married and celibate virtue. The end of life, all human life, is *theosis*. The human person is by nature capable of pursuing that end, and all practices and sustaining virtues may be examined in its light. The narratives of God's love for beings created to share his life, but free also to reject that life, are central to the weighing of various systems of virtue.

We may conclude that an Orthodox Christian virtue ethic for marriage reflects and contains the same *telos* as is found in other areas of Orthodox Christian thought. The same community is found, and marriage no less than monasticism is shown to be a fundamentally ecclesial entity. It may be the case that nuptial asceticism is more fundamental than is celibate asceticism— or images of power and hierarchical control—in envisioning the church. The church as "nuptial" is not essentially a rejection of the world, neither is it a force that subdues, but a love that endures. Christian virtue is revealed here in a fundamentally positive and noncoercive light. The preferred mentors of Orthodox Christian marriage have traditionally been religious celibates. While I find no systematic objection to the use of celibates as mentors, it seems clear that the text of the marriage rite envisions mentors with a practical experience of marriage just as mentors of the monastic way in *The Ladder* are expected to be experienced in that particular practice. The narratives of marriage prove to be those stories of women and men who together find God in the rich matrix of communion in the flesh. The display of virtue which results, while the product of a distinguishable practice, is essentially indistinguishable from the virtue of the monastic as displayed in *The Ladder*.

NOTES

1. John Chrysostom, *Homilies on First and Second Corinthians*, in *A Select Library of Nicene and Post-Nicene Fathers of the Christian Church*, Second Series, vol. 12 (Peabody, Massachusetts: Hendrickson Publishers, Inc., 1994), 131, (*First Corinthians*, homily 13). Elsewhere, in homily 16 on Ephesians, he goes so far as to maintain that it is not even enough to abandon vice. He asks if a servant is good who does not steal, but will not work? Is a tenant farmer what he ought to be if he does not plot against the landlord, but will not prune the vine? No, Chrysostom insists, we need not only abandon evil practices that have no end, but we need to acquire the good habits and dispositions of the "new man." John Chrysostom, *Chrysostom: Homilies on Galatians, Ephesians, Philippians, Colossians, Thessalonians, Timothy, Titus, and Philemon*, in *A*

Select Library of Nicene and Post-Nicene Fathers of the Christian Church, Second Series, vol. 13 (Peabody, Massachusetts: Hendrickson Publishers, Inc., 1994), 125–128 (*Ephesians*, homily 16).

2. John Chrysostom, *First Corinthians*, 132, (homily 23).

3. Ibid., 136.

4. This sentence serves to concisely formulate the task of ethics for theologians as widely separated and unknown to one another as the well-known Stanley Hauerwas and the little-known late (d.1979) Serbian Orthodox scholar and mystic, Justin Popovich. In agreement with John Chrysostom, among others, Popovich also maintained, in *Orthodox Faith and Life in Christ* (Belmont, Massachusetts: Institute for Byzantine and Modern Greek Studies, 1994), 86, that to profess to be an Orthodox Christian is "to be part of the continuous struggle that leads from man to God-man, that is, to be involved in the unending improvement of oneself through the theanthropic mysteries, struggles, and virtues."

5. *First Corinthians*, 74 (homily 13).

6. Chrysostom along with the other Greek Fathers held, according to John Meyendorff, that "Christ, being True God, also manifested a true humanity, not in spite of His divinity, but precisely *because* He was True God: in Him, we see divinity as the true norm of humanity." *Marriage: An Orthodox Perspective* (New York: St. Vladimir's Seminary Press, 1975), 20.

7. *First Corinthians*, 74 (homily 13).

8. Ibid., 76.

9. John Chrysostom, *On Marriage and Family Life*, 42 (*First Corinthians*, homily 19).

10. Paul Evdokimov, *The Sacrament of Love* (Crestwood, New York: St. Vladimir's Seminary Press, 1985), 28.

11. Ibid., 47.

12. Ibid., 45.

13. Stanley Harakas, "Sources in Orthodox Christianity for Bioethical Decision-Making," *Diakonia* 24 (1991): 109–120, at 119.

14. Ibid., 118.

15. *The Sacrament of Holy Matrimony* (New York: The Orthodox Church in America, 1992).

16. Evdokimov, *Sacrament of Love*, 152.

17. Meyendorff, *Marriage*, 38.

18. *Holy Matrimony*, 8.

19. *Marriage*, 27.

20. *Holy Matrimony*, 23.

21. Ibid.

22. Gen.41.41–42.

23. Dan.6.17.

24. Dan.13 in the Septuagint.

25. Gen.38.

26. *Marriage*, 41.

27. *Ephesians*, 114 (homily 13).

28. *Marriage*, 78.

29. Ibid.

30. Ibid., 45.

31. Ibid., 35.

32. The eucharistic liturgy of St. Basil employed by Orthodox Christians requires the priest at the anaphora to pray over the gifts which are identified as the antitype of the Body and Blood of Christ.

33. *Sacrament of Love*, 68.

34. *Holy Matrimony*, 13.

35. *Incarnate Love*, 79–81.

36. John Zizioulas, "The Eucharist and the Kingdom," part 3, *Sourozh* 60 (May 1995): 32–46, at 45.

37. Ibid., p. 44.

38. *Sacrament of Love*, 164.

39. Ibid.

40. *Ephesians*, 144–145, (homily 20).

41. *Marriage*, 22.

42. Ibid.

43. *Sacrament of Love*, 67.

44. *Ephesians*, 97 (homily 9).

45. *Sacrament of Love*, 171.

46. *John Climacus: The Ladder of Divine Ascent*, 172 (step 15).

47. *Ephesians*, 116 (homily 13).

48. *Ephesians*, 130 (homily 17).

49. *Ladder*, 226 (step 25).

50. *Ephesians*, 115 (homily 13).

51. *Sacrament of Love*, 120–21.

52. Ibid., 82.

53. Ibid., 83.

54. Schmemann, *For the Life of the World*, 90.

55. Ibid.

56. Ibid., 82.

57. *Ladder*, 91 (step 4).

58. Ibid., 92.

59. Ibid.

60. *Holy Matrimony*, 13.

61. *Ladder*, 120 (step 4).

62. *Holy Matrimony*, 2.

63. Ibid.

64. Ibid.

65. Ibid., 28.

66. *Ladder*, 286 (step 30).

67. *Life of the World*, 91.

68. *Ladder*, 251 (step 26).

69. Ibid., 287 (step 30).

70. *Life of the World*, 90.

71. *Ladder*, 264 (step 27).

7

Conclusion

Stanley Hauerwas has written that his only project is "to foment a modest revolution by forcing Christians to take themselves seriously as Christians." [1] He has gone about this task by uncovering the cultural-linguistic distinctiveness of Christianity. In Wittgensteinian fashion, he has attempted to free Christians from the entrapments of language, especially the language of the Enlightenment. My work was prompted largely by reading Hauerwas. Taking his lead, I have attempted to follow virtue to see where it would lead me in the Christian East. I discovered that Orthodox Christianity is an incomparable resource for a virtue ethic. At every turn in the rich corpus of Orthodox Christian thought can be found a new opening for a comprehensive virtue ethic.

In a collection of essays published in 1981, Stanley Hauerwas was already responding to what would become—and still is—a persistent criticism of his work. It has about it an unfinished character deriving from his failure to assemble a comprehensive position. [2] He has promised that he would in the future produce a short work to remedy that lacuna. He has not done so, and his work has continued to be ad hoc. At the beginning of this text, I indicated that I would make a modest contribution to virtue ethics by suggesting where an Orthodox Christian virtue ethic might be situated. Whatever has prevented Hauerwas from locating his work in a comprehensive vision, an Orthodox Christian virtue ethic would need to locate its claims in a comprehensive vision that included a lively appreciation of Orthodox Christian tradition, church history, doctrine, spirituality, ecclesiology, worship, the saints, the Scriptures, and God's creation. This is so not because it is necessary to assemble an encyclopedic argument that satisfies any rational inquiry—the Enlightenment project rejected by MacIntyre and Hauerwas—but because the "fellowship of life" extends to and includes all of the saints through all of the ages. An Orthodox Christian virtue ethic must be able to defend and explain itself before John Climacus as well as more "present" voices.

Hauerwas—in a passage that, again, produces profound resonances with Orthodox Christian thought—maintains that Christians confess belief in "church" because it is not simply the Sunday gathering of like-minded individuals but God's creation.[3] He insists that "the worship of God to be appropriately 'appreciated' requires masters located within the company."[4] "Christianity is," he continues, "the name given that company *across the generations* [italics mine] that have learned from one another the skills necessary for the worship of the God known in Jesus Christ."[5] It is because Orthodox Christianity profoundly agrees with all of these claims, that any Orthodox Christian virtue ethic must be able to demonstrate living continuity across the generations. An Orthodox Christian virtue ethic will be different because it must—and, as demonstrated, is fully able to—relate virtue to the whole of the tradition. The weave of Orthodox Christian spirituality is so tightly interwoven with doctrine, liturgy, etc., that one cannot tug one thread without affecting the entire tapestry.

A basic outline of an Orthodox Christian virtue ethic may be found in many places. In a text that we did not explore, Gregory of Nyssa maintains that the good at which we ought to aim is God himself.[6] God is our end and we are free to grow in God's likeness. Human perfection is found in striving after virtue (31 [1.10]). "We are," he insists, "in some manner our own parents, giving birth to ourselves by our own free choice in accordance with whatever we wish to be, whether male or female, molding ourselves to the teaching of virtue or vice" (55–56 [2.3]). "We place ourselves in whichever sphere we wish to be" (72 [2.80]). Yet, we cannot do without guides and exemplars for Christian virtue (32 [1.13]). Christian narratives are needed to display reality aright:

> Just as at sea those who are carried away from the direction of the harbor bring themselves back on course by a clear sign, upon seeing either a beacon light raised up high or some mountain peak coming into view, in the same way Scripture . . . may guide again to the harbor of the divine will those adrift on the sea of life with a pilotless mind (32 [1.11]).

Nyssa does not simply reject the non-Christian world: "There are certain things derived from profane education which should not be rejected when we propose to give birth to virtue" (62 [2.37]). However helpful and laudable such "learning" may be, it is never enough. The world stands in need of meaning. Whatever virtue can be gained "outside" of the church "is always in labor but never gives birth" (57 [2.11]). Christians have but one *telos*: "to be called servants of God by virtue of the lives we live" (135 [2.415]). Christians, Gregory of Nyssa holds, do not strive for virtue because of either punishment or reward,

> as if cashing in on the virtuous life by some business-like and contractual arrangement. On the contrary, disregarding all those things for which we hope and which have been reserved by promise, we regard falling from God's friendship as the only thing dreadful and we consider becoming God's friend the only thing worthy of honor and desire. This, as I have said, is the perfection of life (137 [2.320]).

For Gregory of Nyssa as for all of Orthodox Christianity, the emphasis on virtue is not simply a rejection of minimalist conceptions of human beatitude but the firm conviction that "just as the end of life is the beginning of death, so also stopping in the race of virtue marks the beginning of the race of evil" (30 [1.6]). The human person is forever dynamic, always reaching out. Virtue, therefore, is not a matter of supererogation, but, as presented in the Orthodox Christian tradition, one of only two possible directions. The most essential distinction found in an Orthodox Christian virtue ethic is not between the Kingdom and the world, but between life and death. The world will be made new, but death will be destroyed. Virtue is the pursuit of life and, thus, the putting to death of all that is not of God. It is the recreation of life and, so, of the world as sacrament.

However unabashedly distinctive any such ethic must be, there is also an area wherein it may be said to be commensurable with other understandings and shared by those who are not confessedly Orthodox Christians. There is available from within the Orthodox Christian tradition an appreciation of and call for human excellence that very much resembles that of the late Jewish theologian Abraham J. Heschel, described in chapter 1. Any society must distinguish for itself, as Heschel demonstrated, between mere "human being" and the more of "being human." In a passage that parallels the thought of Rabbi Heschel, John Climacus maintains that there is available in any human community a sort of natural virtue that is not to be despised. The end of such virtue is to negotiate communal life. These virtues distinguish human community from mere animality. Such human sensibilities as showing "mercy" for one another and the sort of "hope" engendered by learning to work together are applauded by John Climacus. [7]

The virtue ethic that I have described—and especially that of John Climacus or Gregory of Nyssa, outlined above—maintains the positive and optimistic view that the end of all human excellence is love, that God is revealed in and as love, and that this love is for all. I agree that "Christianity for Climacus is a natural, human, reasonable and optimistic experience of God's friendship, which is the foundation of the Unity of Mankind." [8]

In summary, there is a virtue ethic peculiar to Orthodox Christianity that is distinctive and not readily accessible to others without catechesis and conversion. Yet, it is not so distinctive as to be completely incommensurable with other Christian—even non-Christian—understandings of virtue. As evidence of this last assertion, I offer the journey of virtue as described by John Climacus. The teachings of *The Ladder* are in the main accessible to Christians, Protestant or Catholic.

Perhaps virtue will yet prove to be not only a rich hermeneutical key for the understanding of Orthodox Christianity, but a resource for uncovering the deep grammar of Christianity, thus allowing a reordering of Christian ecumenism. The literature of virtue ethics has already opened an area of dialogue for Christians of all sorts. John Climacus demonstrated the order of the virtues to require that one learn to love the other *before* one is able to love God. Worship is the very heart of the Christian life, yet even before prayer is love of the neighbor. From very high on the ladder—no less than the twenty-sixth step—John Climacus cautions that if someone comes to ask a question and in so asking disturbs one's prayer, then even prayer ought to be stopped because love is greater than prayer. If Orthodox Christianity is properly characterized by virtue and if John Climacus is correct in insisting that "love is greater than prayer, since the latter is a particular virtue while the former embraces all virtues," [9] then we may with confidence conclude this study by insisting that any Orthodox Christian virtue ethic, however particular and exclusive it is, may never be so exclusive as to preclude dialogue. The "Fellowship of Life" is God's creation, and all are called to the assembly.

NOTES

1. Stanley Hauerwas, *In Good Company: The Church as Polis* (Notre Dame: University of Notre Dame Press, 1995), 12.

2. Stanley Hauerwas, *A Community of Character* (Notre Dame: University of Notre Dame Press, 1981), 6.

3. Hauerwas, *In Good Company*, 9.

4. Ibid.

5. Ibid.

6. Gregory Nyssa, *The Life of Moses*, 31 (*De vita Moysis* 1.7).

7. *Ladder,* 238–239 (step 26).

8. Constantine Tsirpanlis, *Introduction to Eastern Patristic Thought and Orthodox Theology* (Collegeville, Minnesota: The Liturgical Press, 1991), 196.

9. *Ladder,* 239 (step 26).

Index